The Labor of Love

CREATING AN ENDURING
ROMANCE IN YOUR MARRIAGE

TIMOTHY L. HALL

kregel
RESOURCES

Grand Rapids, MI 49501

The Labor of Love: Creating an Enduring Romance in Your Marriage

Copyright © 1996 by Timothy Hall

Published by Kregel Resources, an imprint of Kregel Publications, P.O. Box 2607, Grand Rapids, MI 49501. Kregel Resources provides timely and relevant resources for Christian life and service. Your comments and suggestions are valued.

Cover design: Joe Ragont
Book design: Nicholas G. Richardson

Library of Congress Cataloging-in-Publication Data
Hall, Timothy
    The labor of love: creating an enduring romance in your marriage / Timothy Hall.
        p.   cm.
    1. Marriage. 2. Marriage—Religious aspects—
Christianity. 3. Love. 4. Intimacy (Psychology). I. Title.
HQ734.H2554   1996   248.4—dc20   96-10335
                                                                          CIP

ISBN 0-8254-2848-3

Printed in the United States of America
1 2 3 4 5 / 00 99 98 97 96

To my Darling Husband on our
4th Anniversary

You are my dreams come true...
You fulfill me give me above
and beyond my expectations.
Thanks for your faithful, consitent
love.

Rejoicing for the years God's
given us + hoping for many more
I love you.

For Lee.
My heart is satisfied within the shelter of your love,
desires fulfilled, and wishes granted.
I am content.

Contents

Preface

or half a century, committed love has been on the decline. We have watched a generation experiment with disposable love, leaving a trail of litter and brokenness in its wake. We've realized that the only love worth having is love that lasts, not the easy-come-easy-go variety. But how do we hold on to love? In a world where little seems to last very long, how do we make love stay?

Not by discovering some secret, I'm afraid. There aren't any magic words to make love last, no abracadabras. You will find no secret recipe tucked between the pages of a marriage book or revealed on a talk show. You certainly won't find any revolutionary secrets in this book. What you will find is a fact that you probably know or suspect already: Making love last takes work. *You must work at love to make it last.*

Steadfast love in our time is not a dying art—it is simply a neglected task. Enduring love has suffered in this generation mostly for lack of effort. Of course, it's not that we don't know how to work at it. We can work hard enough when it suits us or when we perceive the necessity. We are workaholics about our careers but not about our loves. We are devoted to gardening and golf, to television and paperback novels, but not to love.

To recapture a lifetime love we must rededicate ourselves to a lifetime labor in love's service. There is no other way, no secret time-saving device waiting to be discovered. There is only the work of lovers who purpose to hold on to love and the work of God, without whose labor, the psalmist declares, the builders of a house labor in vain (Ps. 127:1). This is a book about that work, that labor—the labor of love.

1

Making Love Stay

*N*othing much lasts anymore. Everything is disposable or replaceable: use it up, wear it out, throw it away. Our lives are filled with the clutter of broken things that no longer work, and it doesn't surprise us. After all, who expects more than a twelve-month warranty on anything these days? We have forgotten what permanence looks like—if we ever knew.

Love seems to be as disposable as everything else. We often expect it to wear out like cheap clothing. If all the things we lay our hands on are destined to wear out or break, how can we hope for love to be any different? The news that another marriage "just didn't work out" causes us no more surprise than hearing that a lightbulb needs to be replaced. Brokenness and disrepair are sure beacons of our time. We've lost confidence in having a durable romance.

We complain, of course. "They don't make 'em like they used to," we mutter when the television, VCR, or compact disc player stops working. Maybe we're right. Maybe things used to last. Maybe there was a time when people knew that things didn't last unless they were *made* to last.

Have you noticed that no one ever says, "*We* don't make 'em like *we* used to"? Someone else is always to blame for shoddy work, not us. When something breaks, the fault invariably lies with someone anonymous. *They* failed to do the job right.

Who do we blame, though, for love that doesn't last? Who do we blame when *we* stop loving?

On our first wedding anniversary my wife and I were still in school. Lee needed nine months to finish an undergraduate degree in speech pathology; I had just begun two years of graduate work that would be followed by law school in Austin, Texas. She was twenty years old; I had just turned twenty-two.

A year had passed since our wedding. A good year. We had acquired a cat and had lost one or two wedding presents courtesy of our cat's curiosity. We had finished writing thank-yous for wedding presents and settled into the pleasant rhythm of newly married life.

This one particular day was like most of our days. We left our apartment together early and headed to the car. A day of school and two hours of driving loomed ahead. The first pale breath of winter hovered over the December morning as we weaved our way through the puzzle of cars in the parking lot. We walked in silence at first, but Lee spoke before we reached our car. And I was barely awake when she said the words that seemed to come sixty years too soon.

"Do you know that I still love you?"

I remember whirling toward her, incredulous, forgetting school and traffic. We had only been married a year. "What did she expect?" I wondered, suddenly wide awake. I asked harshly, "Wasn't that the basic idea?" I was surprised and more than a little confused. My wife might as well have confessed to being a Russian spy or a secret mud-wrestling fan. She wouldn't have astonished me any more than she did at that moment.

How could she *not* still love me? I was a decent husband. I listened attentively when she talked, at least most of the time. Although I was not fanatical in the area of neatness, I wasn't a complete slob. We had argued some, but made up quickly. I had remembered both her birthday and our anniversary, never abandoned her on weekends for golf or hunting, never betrayed or beat her. How could she not still love me?

Lee tilted her face toward me, morning light sparkling in her eyes and wind tugging on her long brown hair. Although she smiled with pleasure, her face was full of seriousness rather than mischief. This wasn't a joke, I realized. Something important had happened, some crucial discovery made, like someone finding the missing portion of a treasure map. For her, it was as though a landlord had suddenly granted our love a new long-term lease. In the end her obvious delight soothed my wounded ego. The days and weeks that followed helped to smooth the rough edges of what still seems to me to be a fairly strange way of looking at love and marriage. But for Lee, I discovered, we had arrived at a turning point.

A year earlier she had stood at the altar and said, "I do." When she mingled her vows with mine and spoke those two words that catapulted each of us into a new life, she promised that she would be my wife as long as we both lived. The words "I do" were a solemn vow, spoken reverently. But observation had led my soon-to-be wife to a conclusion of which I was unaware as we stood together on our wedding day. She believed with unshakable confidence that our love could not survive marriage. Lee loved me, of course, with all her heart. She expected love to die, though, once we trapped it inside of our wedding vows. She had watched many marriages around her die—those that dissolved in the acid of divorce and those that woke each morning to bitterness. And, as a watcher of marriages before she became a wife, she entered our union with no expectations that love would thrive there. What was for me a wedding ceremony was for her a kind of funeral service for love, somewhat in advance of its dying. The wedding march that bore her down the aisle toward me, radiant and beautiful, sounded in her ear like a requiem.

When Louis XVI married Marie Antoinette, Louis's father bestowed on their marriage a dubious blessing. "Marriages," he said, "are never happy, but they are sometimes pleasant; let us hope that this one will be." When Lee married me, she had equally unsettling expectations. She didn't expect either love or real happiness to last very long. She simply hoped that the years of our union would be pleasant.

A year later, though, she awoke with wonder to the realization that our love had not died. She discovered that it had flourished and grown. Instead of withering, love had put down deep roots.

Although I stumbled over Lee's words to me that morning, her obvious joy and astonishment moved me to think again about love. Perhaps I had taken it for granted. I had simply assumed that love was a husband's due and was carelessly confident that it would last as long as the rings we exchanged, maintenance-free. Lee reminded me, though, that lovers have to hold on to love and recreate it out of everyday life. Love's continued presence in our lives was for her, and came to be for me, a thing to behold in awe. How did I deserve this? How could my clumsiness not have crushed it?

We did not know so clearly then, as we do now, that love's survival in our marriage was not a complete mystery. We had done many things wrong, but also some important things right. Right enough, at least, to keep love alive. We had begun building a house for love, though we did not recognize it at the time. We had laid a foundation and erected a frame that would house love for a lifetime. The building required work from each of us. For that first year we accomplished many of love's labors without knowing what we were doing. The months and years that followed found us building with more deliberation, becoming gradually more acquainted with the tools of construction. The steady work of love began there, though, in that first year which climaxed in the discovery: *I still love you.*

When Lee and I married, we were not completely unprepared to craft an enduring love. We had dated one another for four years and were inseparable companions during the tumultuous transition from teenagers to adults. We knew each other's secrets and were not blind to each other's faults. Toward the end of the years we dated, we broke up nastily and then rebuilt our relationship after coming close to walking away from each other for good. Our new relationship was stronger, and we meant it to last—no exceptions, no reservations. By the time we reached the altar, we both shared a firm conviction that "till death us do part" was not simply a sentimental cliché appropriate for the country church where our wedding took place. It was a weighty vow not to be taken lightly and not to be broken. We knew, or thought we knew, what we were getting into. Having gotten in, we planned to stay.

In other crucial respects, though, Lee and I arrived at marriage with little training for the task of creating a lasting love affair. We were accustomed to the romances of television and movies, love affairs crammed into an hour or two of screen time—Humphrey Bogart and Katherine Hepburn in *The African Queen* or Tom Hanks and Meg Ryan in *Sleepless in Seattle*. The compact history of film could show little more than an initial flirtation. It rarely suggested more than the first flower of romance.

The hurried romances we saw on the silver screen left us ill-prepared for the less glamorous labor of love, the labor that inhabits a home where two real people live even after the house lights go up and the credits have stopped rolling, the kind that endures sickness and boredom and dirty laundry.

Bogart and Hepburn were little help to us here.

The lessons we ultimately learned about sustaining love over a life-time had almost no parallel to the Technicolor lives we saw on the screen. We learned to talk with each another, to converse even after we had displayed our respective secrets during the first blush of romance. Even after lovers exhaust their secrets, love must still speak. We learned to fight. We did not escape the battles of will or the conflicts of mutual tiredness and frustration. Somehow, though, even while grappling with one another, we managed not to destroy the fragile furniture of love. We learned to protect love from those who wanted to steal it and to guard love from the creeping lethargy to which all life is prone. We locked doors and installed alarm systems.

The lessons we learned began with the discovery that love can be made to stay, and, equally important, that it *must* be made to stay.

In the spring of 1983 Lee and I signed a contract to buy our first house. I was a month shy of finishing law school at the University of Texas, planning to work for two law firms during the summer and to begin work for a federal judge in the fall. After more than five years of apartment living, we were anxious for space. So we contracted to have a tract house built on half an acre of land outside of Austin.

The house was three months in the building, and we visited the site nearly every day to watch the progress. We came mostly in the evenings after the construction crew had left for the day. But we didn't imagine that the slab and plumbing and framing that soon appeared had come from nowhere. It takes builders to build a house. We knew, without seeing, that our house grew up out of the soil because someone was working at it during the day.

Enduring love is like a house—it doesn't spring up overnight by magic. It has a beginning, of course, like the workers pour a cement foundation. It becomes a place capable of weathering wind and rain only because someone, day by day, labored at its building. It takes form over the days and weeks and years, becoming ever more a shelter from the wind and storm, ever more a harbor for those who dwell within its walls.

Lovers, of course, do much of the building, but their labor is not enough to secure success. "Unless the LORD builds the house," the psalmist declared, "its builders labor in vain. Unless the LORD watches over the city, the watchmen stand guard in vain" (127:1). The psalmist began this hymn to the Lord's providence over the home by affirming the necessity of the Lord's labor and of His watchful care. No one can be either successful or secure without the Lord's success and His security. He is the general contractor and head of security for successful homes. We must be careful, though, not to stumble past the assumption implicit in this passage. Building houses requires labor and guarding a city requires watchfulness. The Lord's building and watching are required, but also the labor of human hands and the watching of human eyes.

Most of us have no difficulty recognizing the necessity of steady labor at our jobs. Our employers hover about in case we forget. Time cards chart the hours we apply to labor; salary increases reward persistent work. Morning by morning we settle into the rhythm of work. Day by day we labor in factories, offices, and work sites to make or sell or repair or serve.

At night, though, we return home, tired from the day's labors, anxious for rest. We put work behind us, at least after cooking supper, washing dishes, and putting the kids to bed. Perhaps we work so hard on the job that we resist the idea of anything remotely resembling labor at home, except the work necessary to keep the household going. We expect to find a haven of leisure and rest at home. We shun exertion, celebrate relaxation, and gather around the television.

Our needs and problems don't go away. And sometimes we forget that the needs and problems of our private lives can seldom be solved by anything other than, well, work!

The prospect of more work is not a happy one for minds and bodies already worn out by paid labor. We have our share of problems, and these cry out for solutions. Yet we cling tenaciously to the dream that we can purchase these solutions at a spectacular discount. We are all looking for the diet that will not require us to change our eating habits, for exercise programs that will not trouble us with tiredness or sweat, for relationships that make no demands on our solitary selves. "Cast your bread upon the waters," says Ecclesiastes 11:1, "for after many days you will find it again." We, however, want our bread to return to us magically over the water, without ever casting any ourselves.

We know better. The pot of gold at the end of the rainbow is never around to pay the bills.

The law of life is the law of the harvest. "Do not be deceived: God cannot be mocked," the apostle Paul warned. "A man reaps what he sows" (Gal. 6:7). We reap invariably according to the measure of our sowing. The law of the harvest applies to marriage just as it applies to the other areas of our lives. A lasting love does not grow wild. It survives and thrives only in cultivated soil that is carefully tended to, the work of meticulous gardening.

Many a man and woman wake up surprised one cold morning and wonder what became of the fierce blaze that kindled the early days of their love. They stare at one another as strangers. Coolness has replaced fire. Distaste has filled the void left by desire. They shouldn't be surprised. Love is not a trophy to be won once and then simply admired. It is a fire that needs constant fuel or it will burn low and ultimately die.

You must *make* enduring love. Lasting love does not happen naturally but is a thing created by the work of lovers, and, the psalmist declares, by the work of God. It isn't surprising that our generation finds it difficult to understand this. We generally interpret the phrase "making love" to mean nothing more than "having sex." Previous generations saw making love as the multifaceted work of wooing a beloved. Sex might be one culmination of this work, but not the work itself. Making love had to do with words spoken and gestures made that melded two hearts into one. Today, however, making love means nothing more than the passionate coupling of a moment. Making love these days is about *having*, not *making*. It is about having pleasure and momentary release. It is about having—even *using*—another person.

It's time we recapture the words "making love" from R-rated movies and paperback best-sellers. Husbands and wives should be able to say of their lives together, "We've been making love." By these words they should mean something much more than that they have had sex with one another. They should be testifying that lasting love is born of labor and that they have been busy at love's making.

How much labor is required to make an enduring love and to sustain it over a lifetime? I don't have a simple answer to this question, but I suspect that most lovers grossly underestimate the work required by love. They devote endless hours and untold energy to careers and exercise and hobbies. But they relegate the work of love to a tiny corner of their lives, supported only by occasional minutes of time and halfhearted attention. Why do we suppose that crafting an enduring love will take any less time and energy than the other important activities in our lives? It took me most of a summer's evenings and weekends to screen in the back porch of my house. It has taken me countless hours to write this book. Why should I expect to spend less time and effort on the infinitely more serious and important work of building a lasting love?

Normally we judge the amount of labor required of a particular task by the difficulty and importance of the task. We expect to work harder on jobs that are difficult or on those where much is at stake. The labor of love is both difficult and important. Consequently, we should expect love's labor to require more time and energy rather than less.

The labor of love is difficult because the ongoing communion of two individuals in a hectic and self-absorbed world is a daunting challenge. Love itself deceives lovers at first into thinking that love's labor is pure pleasure and no sweat. Under the charm of romance, lovers serve one another without growing tired. They make effortless sacrifices for one another and for their love. Nothing seems hard. Of course, new lovers under the spell of romance really *are* laboring with great energy and attention, although this labor comes easy. Yet romance will not always bless the lovers with the gift of effortless labor and painless sacrifice. Eventually the romantic spell evaporates, and love's labor becomes like all labor—hard and exhausting.

No harm will have been done by the pleasant deceit of romance unless the lovers fail to see that what was done effortlessly at first must still be done though it takes more work. Too often, lovers become convinced that love requires nothing of them except what they are naturally compelled to do. Since these natural compulsions tend to diminish over time, the lovers end up doing nothing to sustain their love. The man who feels naturally driven in the early days of love to practice great courtesy toward his lover gradually abandons courtesy. Unless he has trained himself in the labor of courtesy, he will ultimately neglect to practice it at all. The woman who finds it easy to listen attentively to her husband in the first days of a marriage soon discovers that attentive listening is hard work. If she has not practiced the work of attention, she will eventually find herself never listening when her husband talks with her.

The labor of love is important because our happiness and our children's happiness are bound up in love's survival. But the labor of love is not only important because it is necessary for love's survival. It is important because it is worth doing. The time has come for men and women to recognize that love's labor is noble work. It is work worthy of a life's best energy. We seem to have forgotten what the ancient Greek poet Homer knew: "There is nothing greater and better than this—when a husband and wife keep a household in oneness of mind, a great woe to their enemies and joy to their friends, and win high renown." *High renown.* That is what lovers win who defy the shortsighted champions of career and ambition and money and status, who choose instead the noble labor of marriage, who refuse to believe that lasting love is an impossible dream, who plant their feet firmly on the ground and pledge to do the work of love as long as they live.

Consider what follows, then, as something like news from the front line of one man and woman who have grappled with love and have managed to hold on to it. I can only talk about love by conveying how it has tasted for Lee and me. Along the way I will talk about our life together so far, not because we have reason to boast about our love for one another, but because it is the only love I really know. Here and there I will point to what I have reason to suspect are general principles for all lovers, especially those who are followers of Christ and committed to finding guidance for life and love in the pages of Scripture.

Success will require a renewed attention by all of us to the work of love. There was a time when the prospect of a lifelong marriage was unexceptional. Divorce was relatively rare, marriages relatively lasting. I have no way of knowing how many of these marriages were inhabited by lovers and how many by men and women who simply managed to endure one another because it was expected that they do so. But the day when a lifelong *anything* was the norm has long since passed.

I will warn you at the outset that there are no secrets about love or marriage buried in these pages. We are all in great trouble if the only possibility of sustaining love over a lifetime hinges on anything so rare as a secret. I think our trouble is of a different kind. We are constantly forgetting that love is, and has always been, mostly a matter of work. This book is about the nature of that work.

The following chapters discuss the various tasks required to sustain an enduring love. As we saw in Psalm 127, God's work in the home consists of two primary activities: building and guarding. Unless the Lord builds the house and watches the city, then we build and watch in vain. So we shall consider the labor of love in terms of the tasks needed to *build* love and to *guard* it. Laboring lovers will have much in common with Nehemiah in the Old Testament. Nehemiah and other Jews set out to rebuild the walls of Jerusalem after returning from exile in Babylon. Because there were enemies who opposed the work, Nehemiah and his coworkers labored to build the wall with one hand even as they clutched a sword to defend it with the other.

<hr />

God's work in the home consists of two primary activities: building and guarding.

<hr />

Love also requires both building and guarding. We will first of all consider the work of building love. By this I mean the ongoing tasks that sustain a lifetime love and keep it in good repair. Although these tasks are many, we will consider some of the most important ones. We will then turn to the labor involved in guarding love.

As we will see, love has enemies. A man and woman may labor conscientiously to craft a lasting love and yet see their relationship crumble because they failed to defend their love even as they were building it. There are hands that would destroy or deface what lovers erect. And so lovers must both build and guard. Of course, lovers must look to Him whose guardianship is essential to the safety of their home. Lovers concerned for the safety of their love from love's enemies will make the security of love a matter of constant petition to a gracious God. But while the Lord watches, lovers must also watch. They must fortify the work of their building against vandals.

Perhaps I should say a final word before we consider the labor that love requires. Reading this or another book about marriage is not a substitute for the labor of love. We may accumulate more and more insight into the craft of building love, but the insight is as worthless as hoarding building plans without ever swinging a hammer down on a nail. "If to do were as easy as to know what were good to do," Shakespeare wrote in *The Merchant of Venice*, "chapels had been churches, and poor men's cottages princes' palaces." We live in dilapidated cottages not so much because we don't know what to do, but because we simply will not rouse ourselves to the stern labor of doing it. So read on, by all means, but get ready to break a sweat. Sooner or later you have to put the book down and get to work.

2

What Is This Thing Called Love?

On the eve of manhood, before a crowd of onlookers, I pledged to love my wife. I said the words with the combination of solemnity and exhilaration that inhabits great vows. But I have a confession to make. At the moment I spoke the words that pledged unfailing love to my new bride, I was mostly in the dark about the measure of the oath I was taking. What was this "love" that I had guaranteed for a lifetime, in sickness and health and all the other circumstances that loomed before us? By what power would I fulfill so daunting a promise as this one, this promise of a lifelong love?

Looking back, I see now that I pledged what I did not fully understand. I signed a blank check not knowing what amount might ultimately be written in. Even now, I stumble in trying to fathom the depth of my promised commitment because the vocabulary of my marriage vow was, and is, imprecise.

I promised love. But the word "love" wears a staggering variety of hats. It describes the feelings that man has for a good football game or a woman for a piece of Waterford crystal. The ten-year-old boy speaks of love for his dog; a mother utters the word of her newborn child; and college friends swear undying allegiance to one another under love's banner.

This same word, already pressed into service for a dozen different causes, must also represent the feelings shared by a man and a woman. Even for this use, the word "love" is badly stretched. It must serve duty for infatuated high school sweethearts and veterans of a forty-year marriage. Love describes both the passion shared during the sexual act and the quiet contentment of a husband and wife sitting down to Thanksgiving dinner.

What precisely did I promise when I promised to love my wife? What is the "love" that I committed myself to sustain through the corridor of years? How can I make love stay when I don't even know what it is?

One way of approaching this question is to borrow words from another language to help us understand love's many-sided character. Greek, the language in which the New Testament was written, offers a broader selection from which to talk about love. It will allow us to segregate the various concepts that we must lump together in the word "love." Late in his life, the Christian apologist C. S. Lewis wrote a book about love called *The Four Loves*. His comments about the nature of love guide part of the discussion that follows.

The Four Loves

The Greeks had four principal words for love: *sterge, phile, eros,* and *agape*. Each word represented a different kind of love. The first three are easy to understand and describe three common forms of love: affection, close friendship, and romance or sexual desire. Here are the first three words and their meanings.

> *Sterge* = affection
> *Phile* = close friendship
> *Eros* = romance and sexual desire

Sterge

What we call "affection," the Greeks called *sterge. Sterge* described the love shared by parents and their children, of people for their ruler, or even of a dog for its master. But *sterge* also represented the more mundane love of people familiar with one another, and this understanding is most important for our purposes. *Sterge* is to love what a well-worn slipper is to a foot, or an overstuffed chair to the back. It is the love shared by people whom time has rubbed close and made comfortable with each other. Affection, C. S. Lewis wrote,

> . . . lives with humble, undress, private things; soft slippers, old clothes, old jokes, the thump of a sleepy dog's tail on the kitchen floor, the sound of a sewing-machine, a [doll] left on the lawn. . . . There is indeed a peculiar charm, both in friendship and in Eros, about those moments when Appreciative love lies, as it were, curled up asleep, and the mere ease and ordinariness of the relationship (free as solitude, yet neither is alone) wraps us round. No need to talk. No need to make love. No needs at all except perhaps to stir the fire.[1]

My wife and I love to read. We delight in buying books or borrowing them from a library. *Sterge* is the love I feel for her when we have been wandering separately in some bookstore and I suddenly come upon her, sitting on a stool with her head bowed over a gardening book. *Sterge* is the love that whispers accompaniment on Saturday nights when we sometimes sit with the books we have gathered in a local bookstore and drink cappucino at a table in the cafe upstairs. *Sterge* cushions us on the nights we take our children to the public library and sit with books on the floor in the children's section while our ten-year-old son browses and our four-year-old daughter cuddles up to see the pictures.

Sterge, affectionate love, is the love that smiles at a shared past. Sometimes the smile is a remembrance of pleasure, sometimes the rueful recollection of pain and trouble. But *sterge* softens even the sharp memories and creates of them a comfortable place where lovers can wander together. Lee and I can laugh now about the night our car was submerged by a sudden flash flood in Houston, Texas—how before it sank I tried to push the floating car to higher ground and how we waded home in chest-deep water. There is no one else with whom I share this memory. I can tell the story to friends, but only Lee's eyes dance with mine over the vision of hazard lights still blinking under water as we left our car. *Sterge* has forged this story, and countless others like it, a particular fit between us that is comfortable and easy.

Sterge is the most resilient of the four loves. It is the love most likely to survive persistent neglect. Long after romance has been allowed to flicker and die, *sterge* will accompany a man and woman into middle-age life. They have shared a bed, vacations, and children.

If they have managed to avoid the hurts and bitterness that might have filled their marriage with deep anguish, then time alone will probably bring them *sterge*, or affectionate love.

Phile

Phile refers to the feelings of two people who share a close relationship and who, over time, learn to care for one another deeply. Two sisters might use this word to describe their love for each other, or two close friends. *Phile* is the love of people who say "we." It is what people inside a circle share and those outside do not. It is the love of people who have known one another long enough and closely enough that they begin to define the world in terms of each other and the events they have shared.

Lovers who are also close friends have experienced *phile*. *Phile* finds its nourishment in the long talks when one heart discovers another and when each, thinking itself alone, finds an unexpected ally. It is the love possessed by those who have listened deeply to one another and have heard the sighs and longings that others hurry past. *Phile* links those who have worked side by side at a task or stood together before an oncoming peril.

For Lee and me, *phile* is the love that expresses our common bond as followers of Christ. Within the path of His calling we are brother and sister, sharers of a common devotion to the Risen Lord.

Phile also represents for us the intimacy woven from a hundred cords of shared pleasures and dreams: Bach's unaccompanied cello suites and John Coltrane's saxophone; Dickens' *A Tale of Two Cities*, which we read out loud together, and *Anna Karenina* by Tolstoy; dreaming about writing books and struggling to make our dreams a reality. When Lee and I shoulder together the care and joy of raising children, *phile* accompanies our labor. And when we hover fearful over one of them with a burning fever, *phile* binds us together even in our fear.

Phile is love born of intimacy, and it can die when deprived of that intimacy. Close friends drift apart; sisters leave home and find separate lives. The man and woman who discover *phile* as they become intimate with one another may also witness the death of *phile* if they abandon that intimacy. *Phile* is nurtured on a diet of shared secrets and dreams and hopes. Deprived of that diet, it will perish as surely as a flower will perish for want of sunlight.

Eros

In the Greek language, *eros* is the love that draws its breath from sexual desire and the sweet, aching sting of Cupid's dart. It is romance and passion. If *sterge* is a proselike love, *eros* is poetic, like lines from Lord Byron.

> She walks in beauty, like the night
>   Of cloudless climes and starry skies;
> And all that's best of dark and bright
>   Meet in her aspect and her eyes:
> Thus mellowed to that tender light
>   Which heaven to gaudy day denies.[2]

Eros is the love that rushes in suddenly and takes the heart's breath away. "You have stolen my heart, my sister, my bride," the lover in the Song of Songs moaned, "you have stolen my heart with one glance of your eyes" (4:9).

Eros is the love most familiar to us, yet it is the one that seems most difficult to sustain through long years of careers and mortgages and children. It seems to thrive on a novelty that ceases to exist after the early days of a marriage. Once dull, routine years have robbed a marriage of this spirit of newness, *eros* often lights upon someone other than the partner of our marriage vows. In quest of *eros*, men and women sacrifice those vows in order to find love in some new person's arms, in a new smile, a new kiss, a new caress. *Eros* thus destroys one love in hopes of creating another.

A principal task of lovers is to harness *eros* with faithfulness. It is a task that requires us to forget most of everything we have ever read in best-sellers or seen on a television or movie screen. But we are getting ahead of ourselves. We will talk later of how lovers can prevent *eros* from fleeing a marriage. But we still have to consider the fourth love.

In addition to *sterge*, *phile*, and *eros*, the Greeks had a final word for love. As we shall see, this fourth love—*agape*—holds the key to the labor that enduring love requires.

Agape

Before the New Testament was written, *agape* had been a dull, colorless word in the Greek language. It was similar to our word "like," a drab, ho-hum kind of word. It served only as a weak substitute for the other three loves, the real loves, the loves of substance and meaning.

But something happened to change this.

Several hundred years before the birth of Christ, a group of Jewish scholars living among Jews who spoke more Greek than Hebrew decided to translate the Old Testament into Greek. They did this so that their people, even those who could no longer read the Hebrew language, could still read and study the Old Testament.

As you may imagine, translating the Hebrew Old Testament into Greek was a stiff challenge, made up of many smaller but equally challenging problems. One of these problems was finding a word to translate the Old Testament concept of love. The Old Testament contains descriptions of several kinds of love—the passionate love of a man for a woman and the affectionate love of a parent for a child, for instance. But the chief lover in the Old Testament is God Himself, who chose the nation of Israel to be His people. The translators needed to find a Greek word to describe this love that Jehovah demonstrated for His people and to describe the love He expected His people to return to Him.

As we have seen, the Jewish scholars had no shortage of possible Greek words to use in translating the Old Testament concepts of love. There was a problem, though. None of the principal Greek words for love seemed appropriate for describing the love of Jehovah for His people or the love He called them to return to Him. *Phile*, the love of people who are bound together in close relationships, wouldn't really work. The prophet Hosea recounted God's description of His love as one that leaped over the boundaries of familiarity and kinship. "I will show my love to the one I called 'Not my loved one.' I will say to those called 'Not my people,' 'You are my people'; and they will say 'You are my God.'" (Hosea 2:23). God's love found strangers and made them into His people. *Phile* just couldn't capture this crucial aspect of God's love. *Sterge*, on the other hand, the love of affection, wasn't strong enough to represent God's love. It was too pale and mild a love to describe the love of Jehovah, who protected His people with the strong hand of His might. Finally, *eros* had more problems than *phile* and *sterge* combined. Various pagans had tried to describe the love of their gods in sexual terms, and the Jewish translators were not about to use a word that still reeked of the unacceptable scent of pagan idolatry.

By the process of elimination, the Jewish scholars had narrowed the possibilities down to a single choice—the colorless and unexciting word, *agape*. Suddenly, however, *agape* didn't look so bad. The vagueness of the word became a blessing. Although *agape* had once been a mild substitute for talking about the real loves—*sterge*, *phile*, and *eros*—now it would describe a new kind of love altogether. *Agape* would now represent the love of Jehovah for His people. It would tell the story of a love that sought out Abraham and made him the father of many nations, a love that blessed Isaac and Jacob, a love that delivered the Israelites out of Egypt with a strong hand. *Agape* would become the love that expressed itself in action rather than in mere feeling. *Agape*, then, was the word the Jewish scholars chose to speak of love in the Old Testament.[3]

Several hundred years later, God inspired the New Testament writers to return to the word *agape*. This is the word used in the New Testament to describe God's unconditional love for man. God's *agape* love gave His Son as a sacrifice for our sins, even while we were enemies still brandishing swords in rebellion against Him. "But God demonstrates his own love [*agape*] for us in this," Paul wrote to the church at Rome, "While we were still sinners, Christ died for us" (5:8). Second, *agape* describes our response to God's love. "We love [*agape*]," the apostle John wrote, "because He first loved [*agape*] us" (1 John 4:19). And third, *agape* describes the character of our love for others as a result of being loved by God and accepted by God through Christ. Again, the apostle John wrote, "And he has given us this command: Whoever loves [*agape*] God must also love [*agape*] his brother" (1 John 4:21).

Agape is used in a variety of contexts in the New Testament but always connotates God's love for us, our love for Him, and our love for other people in response to His love. Thus, in the context of marriage, the apostle Paul exhorted husbands to love [*agape*] their wives as Christ loves [*agape*] the church (Eph. 5:25).

Agape love, in the New Testament as in the Old, is a love principally of will not emotion. It is love that acts before it feels.

Marriage and the Four Loves

We have now seen the four loves of the Greeks: *sterge*, *phile*, *eros*, and *agape*. We have also seen how *agape* became the principal word used in the Bible to refer to love, including the love of a husband and a wife. There is a danger of false holiness at this point, however. We may be tempted to conclude that *agape* is the only proper love between a man and a wife. *Agape*, after all, is the most Godlike of the loves. The word *eros*, in fact, is not used anywhere in either the Old or the New

Testaments. But does this mean that Scripture has no place for romance or friendship or affection between a man and woman? Does it mean that Christian men and women must resign themselves to marriages of a holy *agape* love, barren of *sterge*, *phile*, and especially *eros*? Must they settle for prim *agape* and forget about romance? To answer this question we will have to turn back to the Bible. Look this time not just at words but at the pictures of love revealed in the Scripture, particularly at the biblical accounts of *eros*, or romantic love.

Eros in the Scripture

Although the word *eros* appears nowhere in the Greek New Testament or the Greek translation of the Old Testament, the idea of *eros* is not absent. For example, it would be wrong to see the New Testament's use of *agape* to speak of the love between a man and a woman as a limitation of that love to a purely "spiritual" character that has no place for romance or *eros*. It is clear even from the New Testament that married love appropriately includes that aspect of *eros* relating to sexual desire. Paul had frank words of counsel to married couples who wanted guidance on the relationship between their normal sexual desires and their pursuit of a fervent faith in Christ. He urged husbands and wives not to overdo self-denial in connection with their sexual relationship.

> Now for the matters you wrote about: It is good for a man not to marry. But since there is so much immorality, each man should have his own wife, and each woman her own husband. The husband should fulfill his marital duty to his wife, and likewise the wife to her husband. The wife's body does not belong to her alone but also to her husband. In the same way, the husband's body does not belong to him alone but also to his wife. Do not deprive each other except by mutual consent and for a time, so that you may devote yourselves to prayer. Then come together again so that Satan will not tempt you because of your lack of self-control (1 Cor. 7:1–5).

In the Old Testament, romance turns up quite a number of times. For example, there is certainly more involved than mere will and act in the love of Jacob for Rachel described in Genesis 29. Jacob had fled from his home to escape the wrath of his brother, Esau, and arrived at the household of Laban, his kinsman. When Jacob agreed to work seven years for Laban to win Rachel in marriage, the Scripture says that the years "seemed like only a few days to him because of his love for her" (Gen. 29:20). This is *eros*, even if the word is not used. This is romance, before Shakespeare or Lord Byron.

An even more explicit description of *eros*, or romantic love, occurs in the Song of Solomon or Song of Songs. On the surface, the Songs of Songs is about the courtship of a man and woman and their expressions of love for one another. Although numerous Christian and Jewish commentators have hesitated to take the amorous and sensual language of the Song of Songs at face value, a majority of evangelical scholars see this book as essentially a tribute to married love. To understand the Song of Songs in this light should not startle us. We should not be surprised that God would inspire such a book and that it should be incorporated into Scripture. God, after all, inaugurated the first marriage between Adam and Eve. If God did not blush to inspire such language as we encounter in the Song of Songs, we should not blush to take it at face value.

Songs of Songs is about a courtship and a marriage. It is a book of poetry and speaks unblushingly of love. It describes not simply a love of will or act, but a love of deep emotion, intense passion, and earnest longing. Consider these aspects of the love depicted by the Song of Songs.

First, the Song of Songs speaks of a love that is delight itself. "How delightful is your love, my sister, my bride!" the lover speaks to his beloved (4:10). "How much more pleasing is your love than wine." And she agrees. She too declares that her beloved's love "is more delightful than wine" (1:2). "I delight to sit in his shade," she continues, "and his fruit is sweet to my taste" (2:3).

Second, the Song of Songs describes a love that makes the man and woman weak and powerless. "I am faint with love," the beloved murmurs in 2:5 and 5:8. Her lover responds with the confession that a mere glance from her has stolen his heart (4:9).

Third, both lovers in the Song of Songs experience the sense of possessiveness that is one of the hallmarks of romantic love. Over and over, the beloved reiterates the possessiveness of love. "My lover is mine and I am his," she says in 2:16, and she repeats these words again in 6:3, "I am my lover's and my lover is mine." In 3:4, she declares that she will not surrender her love. "I held him and would not let him go." Toward the end of Song of Songs in 7:10, she repeats once again, "I belong to my lover, and his desire is for me."

Finally, the love of the Song of Songs is one that satisfies the heart's deepest cravings and needs. "I have become in his eyes," the beloved boasts, "like one bringing contentment" (8:10).

The love shared by the man and woman in the Song of Songs is a robust one that quickens the pulse and shortens the breath. It is a love that bursts into poetry and swells into song, one that captures the heart and refuses to release it. The love described by Solomon's Song of Songs is one that makes a lover hurry home from work or slip away from friends for an amorous rendezvous. "Take me away with you— let us hurry!" the beloved says to her lover in 1:4. This is *eros*, though the word is never used.

Eros, then, even if not mentioned specially in either the Old or New Testaments, nevertheless has a prominent place within scriptural portrayals of the love between a man and a woman. It is to be expected and desired in a marriage. Its absence should be cause for alarm.

In a similar way, we should expect the love of a man and a woman to exhibit signs of *phile* and *sterge*. The man who cleaves to a woman in marriage should expect that *phile*, the love of close, intimate relationships, will grow. The marriage of two people is a kind of carving out a space in reality where "I" and "they" take the back seat to "we." And time and increasing familiarity should bring a couple the love of *sterge*, the affection born of familiarity.

But where does *agape* fit in?

The Circumstantial Loves

Eros and *phile* and *sterge* each have this in common: They are *circumstantial* loves. These three loves exist and thrive within specific kinds of circumstances. *Eros* owes its existence in large measure to the circumstance of sexual desire, *phile* to the circumstance of intimate relationships, and *sterge* to the circumstance of familiarity. Without these necessary circumstances, romance, intimacy, and affection will not develop.

Not all circumstances will produce or sustain *eros* or *phile* or *sterge*. Some will either preclude the appearance of these loves in all but the rarest instances or assure their demise once they do appear. *Eros*, for example, will wither and wilt in the presence of circumstances that create bitterness. It may exist for a while, bending against the wind of bitterness, but eventually it will shrivel and die. *Phile*, likewise, is vulnerable to external circumstances. Close friends can follow different paths and grow foreign to one another. Disagreement may trigger deep enmity that destroys that sense of "we" that is *phile*'s hallmark. Even *sterge*, the love of familiarity and comfortableness, can gradually disappear in the face of lives lived more and more apart.

Agape, on the other hand, is not a circumstantial love. *Agape* doesn't depend on a particular kind of circumstance for its existence. You might say that it is a hearty love, one that doesn't require coddling and isn't finicky. *Agape* doesn't rely on the spark of sexual desire or the intimacy created by long-term relationships or the comfort of familiarity. It does the work of love even when circumstances seem against love.

In the Bible, we discover that *agape* is the *manipulator* of circumstances. That we were enemies and strangers and rebels toward God did not incapacitate His love for us. He demonstrated His love (*agape*), Paul wrote, in this: While we were still sinners, Christ died for us (Romans 5:8). God makes sons and daughters of strangers on the basis of a love that acts. His love finds circumstances and alters them. It confronts one reality and calls a new reality into being.

This, then, is the crucial role of *agape* in a marriage. Life does not guarantee an endless stream of circumstances that will be hospitable to the growth and continued existence of *eros* and *phile* and *sterge* between a man and a woman. If anything, the opposite is true. Without some intervention, it is almost certain that a marriage will suffer assault from all kinds of circumstances unhealthy to the existence of these loves. The circumstances of financial worry, careers that develop in different directions, children, and sexual temptation all threaten love. Two people need only stand still and wait to be overtaken by circumstances capable of transforming *eros* into distaste, *phile* into enmity, and *sterge* into bitterness.

Agape alone can grasp the circumstances unfavorable to the other loves and either usher them out the door or alter them altogether. *Agape* does not look at life and say, "Whatever will be, will be." It says rather, "Whatever should be, will be." *Agape* creates the circumstances in which *eros* and the other loves can thrive. It tills the soil, waters the ground, and roots out the weeds. *Agape* creates the familiar comfortableness in which *sterge* takes root, the intimacy that sustains *phile*, the romantic atmosphere that keeps *eros* alive. It does not rely upon emotion to energize these tasks. It does the work of love as a matter of will.

The apostle Paul penned the New Testament's most familiar tribute to *agape* love in the thirteenth chapter of his first letter to the Corinthians. The love he describes is a love that is not the captive of circumstance. It is a love that goes on loving even when circumstances stand in its way.

> Love [*agape*] is patient, love is kind. It does not envy, it does not boast, it is not proud. It is not rude, it is not self-seeking, it is not easily angered, it keeps no record of wrongs. Love does not delight in evil but rejoices with the truth. It always protects, always trusts, always hopes, always perseveres (13:4–7).

So what do these words describing *agape* mean in the context of a marriage? How does *agape* override circumstances?

Love is patient

Love doesn't fume when a spouse takes too long dressing for a party or procrastinates about doing some household chore. Love doesn't expect wishes to be granted all at once and isn't surprised when desires remain unfulfilled. Love waits. It doesn't try to change a lover but waits while God works in His own time.

Love is kind

Love comes bearing a cup of coffee in the morning or a bouquet of summer flowers in the afternoon. It stumbles out of bed first to tend to a crying child in the middle of the night. Love is never short of encouraging words. It takes every opportunity to praise its beloved. Love is helpful. It lends a hand when curtains are being hung (with their diabolically small screws!) and proofreads a spouse's writing.

Love does not envy

Love isn't jealous. It rejoices in a spouse's happiness without coveting it. It is filled with contentment in a husband or wife and refuses to cast so much as a single longing glance toward another man or woman. Love never wishes it were somewhere else.

Love does not boast; it is not proud

Love doesn't claim to be perfect. It doesn't ignore its own faults. Love is not condescending in the face of weakness because it sees weakness enough in itself. Love doesn't lord it over a spouse.

Love is not rude

Love doesn't leave dirty socks on the floor or tools lying in the grass. It doesn't ignore a spouse at a party or make a joke at a lover's expense. Love is gracious and well-mannered. It doesn't forget to say thank-you and doesn't eat the last piece of pie without offering to share it with a beloved. Love opens car doors. It rises to kiss a spouse returning home.

Love is not self-seeking

Love looks out for its lover. It thinks about her pleasure first. It strives to give her the first reason to smile or to laugh. The Bible commentator R. C. H. Lenski once said, "Cure selfishness and you have just replanted the garden of Eden." Those who love one another deeply come as close as anyone can to replanting Eden, for they have renounced, so far as is possible, the clutch of selfishness.

Love is not easily angered

Love takes a deep breath before it takes offense. It overlooks a slight and refuses to leap to anger when insulted. Its settled affection is hard to budge. Love doesn't have a temper. It covers a multitude of faults, which, once covered, can no longer inspire anger.

Love keeps no record of wrongs

Love has a poor memory for being mistreated. Love doesn't keep track of who last apologized. It doesn't bring a score sheet of recent wrongs to every argument. Each wrong it suffers is like the first. Love isn't irritable. It doesn't bear a grudge. Love doesn't pay back a wrong; it doesn't retaliate or exact revenge. It doesn't pout or try to punish a spouse in subtle ways.

Love does not delight in evil but rejoices with the truth

Love does not smile at sin, especially at its own. It doesn't see anything cute about having done wrong nor excuse its sin as being "just human." Love rejoices when the truth prevails. It is on the look-out for what is good rather than what is bad. It doesn't revel in criticism but rather seeks out opportunities to praise its beloved.

Love always protects

Love is a strong tower that its beloved can run into. It is a canopy that protects its beloved from the heat of the day. Love never attacks a beloved; it always defends.

Love always trusts

Love isn't cynical. It doesn't leap to suspicious conclusions but expresses confidence in a beloved. It believes a spouse innocent until uncontrovertible proof says otherwise.

Love always hopes

Even when love is betrayed, when every evidence suggests that it is finished, love hopes. It clings to unseen possibilities in the face of ugly realities. It endures toil and pain and grief with unshakable confidence that the Almighty does not slumber but works all things to the good of those who love Him and have been called according to His purpose (Rom. 8:28).

Love always perseveres

Love is like an army which holds a position at all cost. It will not give up. It will not accept defeat. Love goes on protecting and trusting and hoping even though every ally forsakes it. "Love bears," the commentator John MacArthur writes, "what otherwise is unbearable; it believes what otherwise is unbelievable; it hopes in what otherwise is hopeless; and it endures when anything less than love would give up. After love bears it believes. After it believe it hopes. After it hopes it endures. There is no 'after' for endurance, for endurance is the unending climax of love."[4]

Agape and Eros

In a large part, the following chapters give practical counsel for how *agape* is to carry out its work of molding the circumstances of a marriage so that *eros* and *phile* and *sterge* can grow and flourish. Without *agape*, the love of will and action, the circumstantial loves cannot survive. With its willfull attention, the other loves will thrive.

Eros lacks endurance to energize the labor of love over the duration of a lifetime. *Agape* must supply this endurance. *Agape* creates by will and deed the circumstances in which the other loves take root and grow. *Agape* is the most businesslike of the loves. It identifies the work needed in a marriage, sets the alarm to get up on time, and applies itself to the necessary labor. *Agape* doesn't wait for feeling or inspiration any more than you or I delay going in to work until we feel inclined to. We work, and *agape* works, because there is work to be done and because we are responsible for doing it. Sometimes the work comes easy and is full of pleasure. Sometimes it is hard and accompanied by pain. The work must be done, though, and we do it as a matter of will and determination.

... agape is not the end of married love but its beginning.

One further word needs to be said. Just as a successful marriage requires *agape*'s steely love of will and determination, it also must have the other three loves. In a way, *agape* is not the end of married love but its beginning. Marriage was not intended to be a place where the only thing experienced is will and determination. It is not just to be a demonstration of faithful love, but of intimate, affectionate, and even erotic love.

Marriage is a matter of the will, of keeping faith and choosing to meet the needs of one another with the diligence we give to meeting our own needs. But the marriage of man and woman encompasses heart and emotion as well as will. Those who neglect this reality rob themselves of love's fullness.

In the fifth chapter of the book of Proverbs, Solomon counsels his son to avoid the adulterous woman: "Keep to a path far from her, do not go near the door of her house, lest you give your best strength to others and your years to one who is cruel. . . ." (5:8–9). Solomon charges his son to "drink water from [his] own cistern, running water from [his] own well" (5:15). In short, Solomon counsels self-control and the exercise of will to refrain from unfaithfulness. But he does not let the matter rest there. The attention that the son might squander to his destruction upon the adulterous woman, Solomon urges to be showered instead upon the son's wife. She is to be rejoiced in. "May your fountain be blessed, and may you rejoice in the wife of your youth. A loving doe, a graceful deer—may her breasts satisfy you always, may you ever be captivated by her love" (5:18).

Solomon's counsel climaxes with the exhortation, "may you [or let yourself be] ever be captivated by her love." The Hebrew word translated "captivated" can be understood to mean "intoxicated." "Let yourself be drunk on your wife's love," Solomon instructs his son. "Give yourself over to her intoxicating charms." Immediately after Solomon tells his son to be captivated or intoxicated with that son's wife, Solomon asks, "Why be captivated [or intoxicated], my son, by an adulteress?" (5:20).

You may now see the apparent paradox of Proverbs 5. As a matter of will and self-control, the son is to stay far away from the adulterous woman and to devote himself instead to his wife. He is to be *in control* of the sinful desires that could destroy him. But he does not stop there—gritting his teeth in determination, stern with self-denial. Solomon exhorts his son instead to give himself over to be intoxicated by his wife—in a sense to be *out of control*, ravished by, and captive to his wife.

Proverbs 5, then, is not a choice between sober marital faithfulness and adulterous intoxication. It is a choice between intoxications, between two kinds of captivity. To be sure, it is a choice made by a will obedient to God. But having made the choice, the will is joined by heart and emotions to embrace together the intoxication of love.

Agape is love that gives. Perhaps more important, it is love that gives according to the need of its object. Giving flowers to a man who needs bread is not *agape*. In the context of marriage and the agape love to which we are called, we may ask: What is the need of my mate? And among the many answers we may give to this question, the one most frequently omitted, after years have blunted the memories of first love, is this: He or she needs to be loved with the love of the Song of Songs' lover. There are other needs, of course. But the *agape* that provides home and warmth and spiritual encouragement must not draw back from *eros*. *Eros*, left to itself, will flee before the commonplace of waking beside the same person every day. *Agape*, the love that gives unreservedly, must grasp *eros* by the hand and make it stay.

1. C. S. Lewis, *The Four Loves* (New York: Harcourt, Brace, and Co., 1960), 56–57.
2. Lord Byron, "She Walks in Beauty," *The New Oxford Book of English Verse: 1250–1950*, ed. Helen Gardner (New York: Oxford University Press, 1972), 563.
3. *Theological Dictionary of the New Testament*, ed. Gerhard Kittel (Grand Rapids: Wm. B. Eerdmans, 1964), 1:38–39.
4. John MacArthur Jr., *The MacArthur New Testament Commentary—1 Corinthians* (Chicago: Moody Press, 1984), 355.

3

Making Time for Love

*B*efore my wife in flowing gown and I in rented tuxedo clambered up the steps to the altar to be married, we had found a home. A month before the wedding I moved out of my college dormitory into the product of a Saturday's search—a one bedroom apartment in Houston. Since I had little to move in, the apartment escaped the trauma of a full-scale assault of new belongings. I slept on the floor at first. I had a lamp, a table, four chairs, and the few books I had managed to accumulate. Within a few weeks, Lee added her few possessions to mine: a bed, dishes, and plastic étagères. This was home.

Although Lee and I had little money to speak of, we did not seriously contemplate setting up house without a place to live. We needed a home to display the wedding gifts and shelter a cat soon acquired. Living required a home, and we searched one out. Had we not found a home for rent or purchase, we would have built one, I am sure. It wasn't optional.

Love, like lovers, requires a home. Lasting love between a man and a woman is not immune to the weather. It needs shelter, a place to spread out, room to grow. Without such a place, love will grow cold as surely as a campfire steadily rained on will burn low and finally collapse into a pile of muddy ashes.

Yet the man and woman who make elaborate plans for their living together—collecting chairs and table and bed, deciding on a place, putting down deposits—will frequently overlook the necessity of building a home for love. They will rush forward into life as husband and wife without ever a thought or a murmur of protest that love should be left without shelter. And the shelter needed by love is principally this: *time*.

The man and woman make this mistake honestly, because they have—until now—experienced love primarily in the form of *eros*. By the strings of strong emotion and passion, *eros* has taken care of itself by making the man and wife each do its bidding. The lovers did not have to make elaborate plans for when they would be together. *Eros* planted in each of them a longing for this very thing. They snatched every chance to be alone together. They abandoned friends and sometimes even shirked responsibilities for the pleasure of spending long hours with one another. But *eros* does not weather storms well. It needs shelter. Unless a husband and wife reserve and jealously guard a space of time carved out from the hurry of life, love will not survive. Love will take root and thrive under the canopy of time. To be sure, it needs watering and nourishment from other sources, but it primarily needs *space*—a habitat. Without this space, it will be extinguished by a thousand clutching irritations and competing priorities.

A space of time is to love what room is to a home. Love requires room to spread out and create the ties that bind a man and woman together by a hundred strands, to fill up lives with places in which love may rest and sleep and play and work. It needs half-forgotten alcoves and closets where memories are stored. It requires well-worn furniture on which tired limbs can stretch out.

Time for love must be captured from the claims of a hundred other clamoring voices—of work and children and friends and hobbies. Time for love must be guarded against the encroachments of these claims.

"Quality" Time and Real Time

We should begin by eliminating one phrase from our vocabulary immediately: "quality time." We have all heard, and have likely made ourselves, the following announcement: "My husband and I have very busy schedules, but we spend at least an hour of quality time with each other each week."

"Quality time" is the modern euphemism for the pitiful leftovers of lives misspent. After exhausting themselves on careers and hobbies, men and women gather up the crumbs of their remaining time and dole them out to their spouses and their children, like hard crusts of dry bread to the poor. No one should be fooled, though. To nurture a child or craft an enduring love takes *real* time, not just the scraps from an overstuffed day timer. This is because the work of love, whether for a child or a spouse, is *real* work, the kind that consumes *real* time. Love requires time for talking and listening and being together. It thrives on a diet of hours, starves if feed only minutes, even if they are "quality" minutes.

No one, of course, talks much about quality time at work. We know full well that our employers would laugh us straight out the door if we informed them that we had only thirty minutes a day for their concerns but that we would make sure the time we spent working was quality time. They would insist that real work takes real time. They have a right to demand both quality time *and* real time from us. So do our spouses and our children.

Capturing Time for Love

You cannot grow or manufacture time. You can only capture it in one place and move it to another, like flushing a wild animal out of its hiding and transporting it to a safer habitat. Time for love must always come from time for something else.

You may be able to find more than enough time for love crouched behind a television set (or two!) in your home. Television is a harsh god that demands the sacrifice of virgin time on its altar. Those who complain about the content of television programming see only half the danger lurking there. With television's aid we are, in the words of author Neil Postman, "amusing ourselves to death." Prime-time doses of amusement, even of programs suitable for family viewing, are rotting the core of our lives and our loves. They transform men, women, and children who desperately need to be about the business of living and loving into bland spectators of artificial lives and loves. They fill houses with television words instead of words spoken by lovers and parents and children.

Some kinds of work can be done in front of a television as well as anywhere else. As a teenager, I spent more than a few hours seated in front of a television screen with a basket of string beans at my feet and a bowl of peas I had shelled in my lap. Especially around Christmas, my mother frequently forbade anyone in our family to sit down in front of a television without cracking and shelling a bowl of pecans at the same time. But as hospitable as television may be to these kinds of labor, it is not hospitable to the labor of love. Love's labor requires the attention of hearts and minds, and television is a great thief of attention.

It simply isn't enough for lovers to watch television together. The togetherness of television spectators is insufficient to sustain love. Love requires words spoken, eyes watched for the heart's murmurs. When lovers spend time lounged before a TV, there is no silence for words of love to fill, and lovers' eyes are focused on the shimmering images of the screen rather than on one another.

Some of the best advice Lee and I received before we were married was to set up our home, for at least our first year together, without a television. Neither of us had a television of our own anyway, and since we were both still in college, we had gotten out of the habit of watching TV. So it wasn't very hard to take this advice.

And so in the fall of 1977 Lee and I set out to build a life together without the accompaniment of television. We talked and listened and played double solitaire on the bed together. We sat together at the kitchen table with books and paper spread about us. We fought from time to time that first year. And because a television's volume was not available to mask the pungent scent of anger in the air, we quickly made up.

The first year without a television stretched into a second and a third and ultimately more than ten years before we finally bought one. It still sits mostly silent, turned off except for a handful of hours a week. Lee and I both view it as something of an intruder, a thief of hours that belong to family and to love. We have made a tentative peace with the thing, but still post watches to guard our love.

Time for love may also have to be captured from the claims of work. Because Lee and I are not independently wealthy, our principal financial asset is our time. In exchange for sizeable chunks of our daily allotment of time, both of us are capable of finding some employer who will exchange our time for money. We can, in essence, buy money with time. We can then exchange this money for a home and food and cars, for books and stereos and vacations. But our time has other purchasing powers besides its power to purchase money. A passionate, enduring love can only be bought with time. Time buys moments of intimacy and laughter and togetherness. Our time can also purchase happy hours with our children and ministries in the various areas in which God has gifted us. We were taught as children that nothing in life is free. Marriages, happy children, and fruitful ministries can only be purchased with the coin of time.

So what is a lifelong love worth? It must be bought with time, and time used to purchase lasting love can't also be used for anything else. To choose love may well mean foregoing any number of the things that time could buy.

After I had been out of law school for about six years, Lee and I had the opportunity to decide in a very specific way what love was worth. I finished law school in 1983 with a record that allowed me to find a good paying job with a prestigious Texas law firm. Lee and I quickly found ourselves making more money than we had ever imagined possible. She was able to quit the job that had allowed us to survive while I went to law school and busy herself with the occupation of tending children and creating a home. I plunged into the work of a corporate trial lawyer, work I enjoyed and did well. With the money that was now bulging our once tattered pockets, we bought a house and cars and a hundred other things that we had done without during the long, lean years of college, graduate school, and finally law school. My salary, startling to us at the beginning, increased dramatically every year. I had every reason to expect that I would be a partner in my law firm within seven years.

Nothing, though, is free. As an associate in a large law firm, my performance was judged at least partially by the number of hours I "billed" each year. Hours billed are hours spent working on the various legal needs of clients, hours that can be charged to a client, hours from which a firm receives its income. Although my firm had no set requirement for the hours its young lawyers were expected to bill, I knew that my prospects for partnership would be best if I billed at least two thousand hours a year. More would be better. If I were never sick, this meant billing about forty hours a week and taking one week of vacation. But every lawyer works more hours than can be billed to a client: hours spent staying abreast of general legal developments, recruiting law students to join the firm, or (less frequently) doing legal work *pro bono* for clients who cannot afford to pay a fee. On average, billing forty hours a week means actually working fifty-five or sixty hours.

Sixty hours a week over the course of a year is hard work, but certainly not impossible. But these hours and the stress of law practice claimed other hours beyond the ones actually spent at work. When my caseload was low, I fretted that I was not billing enough hours. When a trial was imminent or on especially complicated cases, I often worked seventy, eighty, or even ninety hours a week. When these hours were over, more time was consumed recovering from fatigue. Whether I was stressed out or tired out, I was poor company for Lee. When I came home, it wasn't always easy to switch out of the cross-examination mode in which I regularly lived as a trial lawyer. To be honest, I mostly failed to make this switch. Lee, of course, didn't take well to being cross-examined like a hostile witness at trial.

In any event, my work consumed more hours than I spent at the office. I was out of town frequently. During these periods, Lee and I didn't even have the hour or so before bed that we normally would have had together. This was time we desperately needed to do the work of keeping our lives linked together by making each other partners in the day's events. During the last four months Lee was pregnant with our first child, I spent most of my time in New York and New Jersey working on a large case. I left home each Sunday afternoon and returned late Friday night.

All of these hours were stolen from time needed to build a lasting love with Lee, and they were stolen from our son and from a host of other callings that could only be purchased with time. Lee was gradually beginning to learn to accept a husband's income as a substitute for the husband. I knew my son chiefly by his picture on my desk.

One day in my fifth year of practicing law, with partnership in sight and ever more dollars in our pockets purchased with ever more of my time, Lee and I made a decision. We decided that our love and our son and the callings to which God was bidding us were worth more money than my law firm could ever pay for the irreplaceable time it demanded from me. How much was our love worth? We chose for me to leave the practice of law and become a law professor at half the salary. Our love was at risk, we believed, and we counted it worth more than a beautiful house and cars and clothes. "Better a meal of vegetables where there is love," we learned from Proverbs 15:17, "than a fattened calf with hatred." In our case, a closer reading would have been, "Better a meal of vegetables and love than of prime rib and a law firm partnership."

What did we buy with the time that the practice of law had paid me so well for? Not very much, I suppose, by the calculations of the world in which we find ourselves. We bought evenings where I still work hard but can do so with Lee swinging beside me on a porch swing. For the first three years after we moved from Texas to Oxford, Mississippi, we lived in a small house located on the campus where I teach, a stone's throw away from the law school. Here we managed to purchase for my six-year-old son the ability to walk to his father's office on warm summer days so I could take time to help him read *The Cat in the Hat.* Lee and I purchased the time for me to write this book and for us to brood together over it, to walk to concerts on crisp autumn evenings, to visit new neighbors, to welcome law students into our home.

What is love worth? How much time will we spend to secure our lives from the dying of love, from the creeping coolness that displaces *eros,* from the decaying of *sterge* and *phile?* It is perhaps one thing to buy money with time to meet the necessities of life. It is another to spend time that might have purchased a lifelong love on products with one-year warranties.

Lee and I have pondered over a number of major purchases in our lives so far. But one purchase we plan to make someday, and are saving for now, stands near the top of our list. In one sense, the actual expense of this purchase will be small, but in another sense it will require us to scrimp and save for all our days. It will require us to forego lesser purchases, to do without things that everyone around us is hurrying to buy. Our purchase? Simply this: We are saving up a thousand moments to buy a love that will last as long as the both of us live.

Making Definite Time for Love

In the story of the courtship between two lovers that the Song of Solomon recounts, one of the earliest episodes in the book speaks to the claims of love in relationship to work. "Tell me," the woman says, "you whom I love, where you graze your flock and where you rest your sheep at midday. Why should I be like a veiled woman beside the flocks of your friends?" (1:7).

The labor of making time for love requires planning. Like the lovers in Song of Solomon, those who would capture time for love must not rely on chance meetings or momentary inclinations. The world is a crowded place, and devourers of time lie about on every hand. Lovers must mark out deliberately the boundaries in which time for love will be found. They must plan for love. They must schedule places and times of meeting: "Tell me, you whom I love, where you graze your flock and where you rest your sheep at midday." The time reserved for love must be definite enough to be marked on a calendar.

Remember, as the years pass and the responsibilities undertaken by a man and woman increase, the demands on their time spiral upwards. Work and children and bills consume an ever enlarging portion of their time. If they do not set aside specific time for one another, they will discover that they spend increasingly less time at the work of love.

So what time have you planned for love? For Lee and me, one of love's principal times is Friday or Saturday night (depending on when we can find a baby-sitter). For the eighteen years that we have been married, including the ten years that we have been parents, we have seldom failed to go out on a date a least once a week. Whether we eat out or see a movie or drink a cup of cappucino at a local bookstore, we leave the house and the children and make the time to be together. These dates cost money, of course. Lee likes to think of the money we have invested in going out over the years as the Tuperware sacrifice. Every time she visits someone and sees all the Tuperware dishes filling the cupboards, she reminds herself that the reason she has almost no such dishes herself is that we have spent the money on dates instead. A fair exchange, we think. Of course, different families spend money differently. I am only suggesting that lovers who value their love will scrimp where they can to save money to do things together. If this means scaling back on an expensive hobby or enduring threadbare furniture, the exchange is well worth making.

As the Song of Songs indicates, the creation of time for love is also a public event. By access to her lover's plans for the day, the beloved in Song of Solomon sought an acknowledgment, visible to all her lover's friends, of her place in his life. "Why should I be like a veiled woman," that is, like a prostitute, "beside the flocks of your friends?" she asked. She wanted to be able to visit him, openly and without embarrassment, in the chief places where he lived his life. By this access, love claimed dominion—or at least partnership—with work. Of course, the beloved did not seek a perpetual lovers' hideaway where the lovers permanently abandoned work. Sheep require tending. Bodies must have the food and clothing that labor among sheep provides. But she sought a love that wasn't ashamed of itself, that touched all of her lover's life, even the time spent at work, and was not blocked off into some private place and renounced elsewhere.

The principle suggested here doesn't just apply to sheepherders. All lovers must work at making their jobs subject to love's claim. This means laboring to see that my wife is at home in the place where I work whenever this is possible. I want Lee to be free to drop by my office whenever she wants and to be acquainted with my colleagues.

Her pictures decorate my office. I mention her frequently in conversations with my students and associates. By all these devices, I hope to allow love to penetrate my daily labor.

The Green Chair

Lee and I used to have a study in our house. It was a room with many books, a desk, a computer, and a green velvet chair. The chair sat in front of the desk for a definite reason. You see, we expected that I would probably spend a lot of time in that room—I like to read and write and I'm a "computaholic." But Lee and I valued the relationship that we had built together over the years. We could easily imagine me in the study and her in the living room and our relationship ever more distant.

The green chair was our solution.

In the green chair Lee could do things that could have been done somewhere else, but in the green chair she could do them with me. She could read or sew or write letters while I read or wrote or paid bills. I could ask her to read something I had just written on the computer, and she could read me a quotation from the book she was reading. Of course, when Lee was in the green chair we didn't talk to one another constantly. But there were frequent glances at one another, words spoken, and lives shared.

When our first child, Ben, was born, we converted the study into a bedroom. We moved my desk and the green chair and all of our books upstairs to a large room that had been the master bedroom before we decided to move downstairs closer to Ben. But it didn't take Lee and me long to discover that something about our respective orbits had changed. Now a toddler had to be looked after, and both Lee and I spent most of our time downstairs in our large family room or in the kitchen. The upstairs study, with its desk and green chair, now seemed impossibly removed from the new direction life was pulling us.

But I still had work to do at the desk: bills to be paid, Sunday school lessons to prepare, legal work brought home from the office. And so we transformed the principle of the green chair to our new pattern of life. We moved the desk and the green chair into our family room. This arrangement made poor decorative sense, I am sure. I know that more than a few visitors to our house wondered at the arrangement. But it made all the sense in the world for our commitment to sustain a life together.

We learned two important principles from our early experience with the green chair. First, we discovered that guarding and sustaining love requires attention to the small details of living, details as trivial as where a particular chair will be positioned in a house. Of course, no one detail is likely to determine the course of an enduring romance. But partners who regularly ignore the effect of small matters on their love will find their love ultimately smothered under the collective weight of choices— each in themselves quite insignificant—that collectively strangle love. They may charge into hobbies or sports that take them in separate directions on the weekend. They may succumb to the temptation to involve their children in the host of activities available to them from grade school onwards, even when this requires spending hours of time ferrying children back and forth. They may overcommit themselves at church or in other community activities. None of these things, standing alone, would be much of a threat to love. But piled together, they can easily overwhelm the sturdiest romance.

Second, Lee and I learned to make our possessions the servant of love rather than our being the servants of our possessions. What good is an exquisitely decorated living room if love cannot live there? What good are antiques and cars and stereo systems if they do not contribute to an environment in which love can flourish? The desk in our family room was no doubt unsightly to visitors. But our love lived there permanently, and we were more concerned that it be comfortable than that our guests should think highly of our home-decorating skills.

The principle of the green chair keeps being applied with new results for Lee and me. When I left the practice of law and became a law school professor, we moved into a much smaller house. The family room was too small for my desk. So we moved it into the dining room. Once again, we might have found a place for it in some back bedroom, but it would have acted as a magnet pulling me little by little into a private world even when I was at home.

We learned one final lesson from the green chair. The movement of that chair and my desk through the various houses we have lived in reflects the movement of our lives. We do not stand still. And a love that will survive the progress of a lifetime of days cannot be anchored in one place and simply forgotten about. The labor of making time for love is seldom completed simply by adopting and abiding by a schedule. For Lee and me, and probably for most long-term lovers, life continually rearranges the nature of our commitments. Time for love must be continually captured from these shifting commitments.

Attention

Time is crucial to a lasting love, but it is not enough. Lovers must not only make time for one another and for love, they must focus attention on the labor of love.

My little girl, Amy, is nearly five years old as I write these words, but I remember vividly what it was like when she was two. Her wants were many and insistent. She wanted her shoes on and then off, and then she wanted to wear my shoes or her mother's. She wanted crackers and "ceekies" (cookies). She had an insatiable thirst for milk and apple juice. She needed changing, cuddling, and chasing.

The daily work of living demands not simply that we be present, but that we be focused. It isn't enought to just punch in.

My wife and I had to attend quite closely to what Amy was doing at any given time. We knew that she could, in some time shorter than a blink of an eye, settle down for a feast at the dogfood bowl or pull all the books off the lower shelves in our study. We listened for silence when Amy was out of sight. We knew that silence meant she was busy engaging in some act of infant mischief, mostly of the destructive variety. When we called, she frequently arrived with one of our books in her left hand and a crayola in her right. She smiled and said, simply, "Color!" If we had been more attentive, Amy would not yet have added her own annotations to an expensive book.

This labor of having to pay attention to what Amy needed and did never really took us by surprise, I suppose. We knew from school and work that most important endeavors require not just time but attention. The daily work of living demands not simply that we be present but that we be focused. It isn't enough to just punch in.

A relationship between a man and a woman is something like an infant child in its demand for attention. You ignore it at your peril. Perhaps a lasting love doesn't require quite the moment-by-moment watchfulness that a two-year-old does, but love needs focus as well as time. When love is not attended to for long periods of time, lovers invariably rouse themselves at last to discover that something valuable has slipped away.

The attention required by love is mostly attention to the labor of love that I will discuss in the pages that follow, to all of the ongoing work required to sustain love across the march of time. Yet it is not just the steady focus on the work of love but on the love itself between a man and a woman. Lovers who seek to make love stay will take frequent stock of their relationship. They will ask one another, "Is everything all right?" They will listen for silence and the feelings that silence sometimes hides.

Lee and I have tried to attend to love in this way by frequently asking one another whether the various activities that fill our lives are consistent with our commitment to an enduring love. For example, over the past year, I have spent a fair amount of time in a small workshop behind our house. I have been trying to make small pieces of furniture, and Lee has kept my list of planned projects full of ideas for our family room. Because this work consumed a lot of time and kept me out-of-doors many evenings, I have been concerned that Lee might feel neglected. And so I have asked her from time to time whether she was still happy to have me sawing and gluing and finishing in my little shop. So far, she has always answered "yes." But attentiveness to love requires that I keep on asking, and that if her answer some day changes, I be prepared to change too.

Our decision for me to give up the practice of law in exchange for teaching came after similar conversations. Before we made this decision, we regularly took stock of the way my work was affecting our relationship. We wondered whether being made a partner in my law firm in a few years would change things. We asked one another whether it was worth waiting until then. Now, I don't want to suggest that we were always in agreement as to what we should do. I enjoyed the work of trial law and enjoyed the money that it brought Lee and me. Lee hated the hours I spent away from her. We argued. She cried. I was sometimes frustrated about what to do. But we continued to hold the matter up to one another for consideration and to God for guidance. Ultimately we became convinced that a career change was what our love demanded.

Coming Away

When newly wed lovers charge through a rain of rice or birdseed and stumble into a car decked with cans and shaving cream, they enact

one of love's most important rituals. They escape for a brief
honeymoon, lost to the demands of work and the claims of friends.
They expect to return, though, and set about the business of living.
But this first escape should be precisely that: an escape of many. Love
will require an endless series of such escapes—not on so grand a
scale to be sure, but escapes nevertheless.

We have seen the biblical account of two lovers in the Song of
Songs. It is worth observing that this account both begins and ends
with an invitation to retreat from the rough and tangle of everyday life
to the hidden harbor of intimacy. "Take me away with you," the beloved
entreats her lover, "let us hurry! The king has brought me into his
chambers" (1:4). Later she invites her love to leave the city for a night
in the country. "Come, my lover, let us go to the countryside, let us
spend the night in the villages." Having seen the budding vines and
the blooming pomegranates, she assures him, "there I will give you
my love" (7:11–12). And again, in the last words of the book, she
beseeches once more, "Come away, my lover, and be like a gazelle or
like a young stag on the spice-laden mountains" (8:14).

The lover also knows the necessity of love's escape, and he too
calls upon his beloved to join him in leaving the ordinary business of
life for love's solitude.

> My lover spoke and said to me,
> "Arise, my darling,
> my beautiful one, and come with me.
> See! The winter is past;
> the rains are over and gone.
> Flowers appear on the earth;
> the season of singing has come,
> the cooing of doves is heard in our land.
> The fig tree forms its early fruit;
> the blossoming vines spread their fragrance.
> Arise, come, my darling;
> my beautiful one, come with me."
>
> Song of Songs 2:10–13

"Come away with me" is one of love's chief anthems. Love can
weather work and children and trouble and pain, but it needs regular
holidays, days spent celebrating and rekindling intimacy.

Come away! From television and work and children and friends and relatives. Imagine you have plunged again through a flurry of rice into a fleeing car. Escape from your normal habitat to a quiet restaurant or a tree-canopied hideaway. Leave behind the numbing flicker of television and the sharp demands of your job. Find a baby-sitter to tend the children. Grasp your lover's hand for an out-of-doors walk. Make escape together a regular part of your week. Plan for it. Do not be deterred from it. Come away!

4

Intimacy

*I*n Solomon's Song of Songs, the lover says to his beloved, "My dove in the clefts of the rock, in the hiding places on the mountainside, show me your face, let me hear your voice; for your voice is sweet, and your face is lovely" (2:14).

The labor of intimacy is the labor of showing faces. It is the labor of finding one another in the secret places of our hiding and calling out, "Let me see your face; let me hear your voice." Intimacy is as crucial to love as food is to life. You can starve love by starving it of intimacy. The husband who never listens to the depths of his wife's soul, or never bares the secrets of his own to her, is consigning love to a death that may come slowly but will nevertheless surely come. The wife who never pierces beneath her husband's stoic exterior to feel his heart beat has relinquished love.

The labor of intimacy is precisely the labor to which *eros* drives new lovers. Under the gentle prodding of *eros*, the labor of intimacy is not true labor but the pure pleasure of discovery. Lovers tell secrets, reveal dreams, recount histories. They pull down veils, and man and woman see each other in the pure white light of *eros*.

But the first blush of *eros* ultimately passes, and the intimacy it prompts is not a permanent gift. Without continued labor, intimacy collapses into vague familiarity. This is so because lovers go on living even as they propose to go on loving. They undertake different occupations during the day, meet new people, read new books. They grow, and in growing, change. The intimacy captured at one moment ceases to be intimacy the next because the lovers themselves are partially reborn as strangers each day. They are continually stumbling into new mountainside clefts that hide their faces and muffle their voices from one another.

Lovers who seek to sustain intimacy must learn to recognize when distance has crept between them. Each must be conscious of when the other is absent and be willing to drop everything and find the lover who has become momentarily lost. Solomon's Song of Songs contains a vivid description of the kind of searching that lovers must be quick to launch for one another. At one point the beloved loses track of her lover.

> All night on my bed I looked for the one my heart loves; I looked for him but did not find him. I will get up now and go about the city, through its streets and squares; I will search for the one my heart loves. So I looked for him but did not find him. The watchmen found me as they made their rounds in the city. "Have you seen the one my heart loves?" Scarcely had I passed them when I found the one my heart loves. I held him and would not let him go till I had brought him to my mother's house, to the room of the one who conceived me (3:1–4).

Strangeness and distance will overtake intimacy unless the lovers turn their hands to the labor of showing faces. After the early days of loving have passed, the labor of showing faces is real labor. It is hard. Harder frequently than silence, less comfortable sometimes than loneliness. But love cannot survive without this labor.

The labor required to sustain intimacy is the most important gift lovers bring to one another. No lesser gifts will do. "Rings and other jewels are not gifts," Ralph Waldo Emerson wrote, "but apologies for gifts. The only gift is a portion of thyself."[1] A man and woman cannot starve a marriage of intimacy and then expect to rescue a dying love with yearly anniversary gifts, no matter how expensive they are. Lovers must each give a portion of themselves and receive the portion given by the other.

The intimacy of the sexual act is but a single strand in this larger twisted cord of intimacy that embraces not only our bodies but our hearts and minds and wills. The creeping separateness that challenges love cannot be held at bay by sex alone. The only defense to the separateness that constantly pulls against my marriage bond is a rich intimacy that finds everything I am in the secret clefts of my being and makes it a place where Lee can dwell, that discovers every hope and fear hidden in her and makes them familiar to me.

Talking and Listening

What, then, does the labor of intimacy require of a man and a woman? Chiefly this: Intimacy requires the sustained work of *talking* and *listening*. This is a two-fold labor, and lovers cannot adopt roles that make one of them the talker and the other a listener. Both must talk. Both must listen.

The work of talking and listening requires Lee to speak to me about the things that matter to her and for me to listen. This is hard work for both of us. It is hard for her because she must use precious energy retained after tending two children to help me relive with her the daily triumphs and defeats of that tending. It is hard for me, because I must put aside my preoccupation with work or writing to enter into her telling. The work of talking and listening also requires me to speak with Lee about the things that concern me, to make her a partner in the legal research that fills my days, in the doings of the students I teach, and in the goings on of faculty politics. This work is hard because it requires me to make what has already passed into something present for Lee. It is hard for her because she has preoccupations of her own and because she is called upon to enter, at least partially, into a life that is not her own.

Intimacy requires the sustained work of talking and listening.

And so we talk and listen, about people and books and projects and ambitions. Each word spoken and listened to is like a line cast between two ships, grappling them together. Our aim is to bind ourselves together by innumerable cords so that we do not drift apart. Lee tells me about an article she is writing, about a particularly trying antic of Amy's, or a particular joy of which Amy was the author. I pass her a few pages from this chapter as we sit outside on a sultry Mississippi Sunday afternoon or plot with her the work I will have to do to get tenure at the law school where I teach. She tosses me a line from her life and I anchor it in mine. I launch her a cord from my world and she secures it in hers. Thus intimacy is captured out of the happenings of each day. Like beams joining two walls, our talking and our listening craft the dwelling place of intimacy out of what would otherwise be separate lives. The end of our labor is a single house, two become one flesh.

The labor of talking and listening is one of love's most important labors, and at least for some lovers, one of its most difficult. For those who find talking and listening awkward, the following suggestions might be of some help.

Don't expect instant intimacy, especially of a partner who finds talking difficult. Intimacy is like a car on a cold day: It can use a little warming up before you hit the freeway. Get used to talking about what happened at work today before you start exploring one another's most secret fears or ambitions.

Look for natural opportunities for intimate conversation rather than forced ones. Forced intimacy is asking out of the blue, "What are you most afraid of?" Natural intimacy happens when lovers use things that happen to one another, books they read, movies they see, as a springboard for talking about important things.

Be sensitive about when to expect your lover to be up to the hard work of talking and listening. It is work, remember, at least some of the time. Don't expect an exhausted or harried lover to be in good form for the work of talking and listening. Perhaps the moment your spouse arrives through the door in the evening from work is not the best time for an intimate chat. Yet the exhausted or harried lover cannot use exhaustion or stress as a perpetual excuse to forego the work of talking and listening. Love must endure through exhaustion and through stress. Lovers must talk and listen even when they are undergoing long terms of arduous labor or stress.

A good listener is almost invariably a questioner as well. If you are completely silent while your spouse is talking, you are probably not really listening. Good listeners ask questions; they make sympathetic comments. This is the way they tell their lovers that they are really listening.

Remember that the work of talking and listening requires time and space. Not much intimacy can be squeezed into a television commercial. Turn the television off. Get the kids to bed early. Put on some quiet music. Watch the fire together. Then talk—and listen.

Intimacy and Eros

I have only turned eighteen years old once in my life. I have only graduated from high school once and only once taken a girl out on my first date.

For me, all these events happened when I was a senior in high school. They combined to lend that year a particular flavor that has not been, and probably cannot be, repeated. It was a sweet taste— exotic, and with a certain fizz on the tongue. It was stirred out of circumstances themselves unique, a concoction beyond my power to recreate. It so happens that my first date, my first kiss, and my first love coincided with the woman who is my wife

Eros thrives on novelty. Every moment of those days when I first fell in love with Lee was a new experience. The novelty of those passing moments fueled my love and intoxicated me with the heady aroma of romance. Much of the novelty was in discovering Lee for the first time. I learned to see behind the laugh in her eyes and gaze into the silent place of her heart. We talked and discovered one another, as though we were each adventurers stumbling to the shore of some new continent. But it wasn't just Lee who was new to me. In those early days of loving one another, we fueled the newness of being together with the newness of new places to eat, new songs to listen to and sing, new places to visit. That year our school band went to Chicago for a band festival. Lee and I rode on a train from Houston to Chicago with our band, the first train ride for both of us. We toured Chicago together, a city farther away and more exciting than either of us had ever seen before. We played our first video game together—Pong. Those moments of discovery in Chicago, and others like it at home, fueled our love. They made the passing weeks a continual unwrapping of the unknown and unexperienced together. Every day was like a gift we opened together.

That first year of our love is now more than twenty years in the past. Time has replaced the discoveries we made that year with familiar pleasures. Everything new becomes old and familiar. I have loved Lee as an eighteen-year-old, and now more than twenty years later, as a man with two children. I have caressed her as a husband caresses his wife for the first time, and for the ten thousandth. I am no longer a teenage boy, perched on the brink of manhood, life waiting to be discovered. I am man with a wife, two children, a mortgage, and student loans finally paid off.

If *eros* thrives on novelty, how does it survive in middle age? I can never repeat my first hesitant kiss and recapture its startled strangeness and sweetness. I can never totter again upon the pendulum of delight and dismay in first discovering and alternately doubting Lee's love for me. I can never again ride a train with her for the first time or explore Chicago together for the first time. If *eros* can only thrive in these moments of newness, then Lee and I are doomed to grow old without its presence, comfortable with the love of *sterge* or familiarity, perhaps, bound by the close love of *phile*, but helpless to do more than remember the romance of *eros*.

If *eros* depends for its existence on novelty, then a man and a woman seem to me to have three options. In the first place, they may simply give up the thought of *eros* and romantic love. Despairing of reliving moments that can only be lived once, they may settle for a love of familiarity and closeness and resign themselves to the death of *eros*. They may sit side by side before a television program or watch their children play, committed to faithfulness without romance, tied together by the strength of their marriage vows, but remembering ever more distantly the passion of their youth.

In the second place, fed by a diet of popular books and movies, the man or woman may abandon faithfulness in pursuit of *eros* with someone new. If they cannot repeat the passion of the first embrace with their lover, they may be drawn to repeat it with someone else. Looking for a romance they no longer feel, they will sacrifice *sterge* and *phile* with their lover to whom God has united them and seek to find *eros* in another's arms. They will do so at awful cost to their mate, children, and to God. They will eat the fruit of brokenness and betrayal, and they will make every soul they once counted dear eat of the same fruit.

But a third possibility lies before the man and woman. They can acknowledge the truth. They can never repeat their first kiss or their first embrace, never murmur love again for the first time to one another. There is, I admit, a certain sadness in this truth. But it is like the sadness in the brief interlude after you have read one good book and before you have begun another. It is the sweet regret of finishing a fine salad a few moments before the main course is served. We naturally desire to repeat pleasure in the form we first experience it, but this is a desire that God does not always, perhaps not even frequently, fulfill. "It would be rash to say that there is any prayer which God *never* grants," C. S. Lewis once wrote. "But the strongest candidate is the prayer we might express in the single word *encore*."[2] While we gaze behind, hoping for a glimpse of that which is past, He calls us forward to the future.

We know this well enough some of the time. We don't expect a constant repetition of the past, even when it holds great pleasure. The rule of life is growth, not repetition. Every parent is constantly reminded of this rule.

A few weeks before my son turned six I took the training wheels off his bicycle. At the time, we lived beside the law school where I teach, so with the newly liberated bike we walked to the law school parking lot. My son, Ben, put his feet on the pedals, I grabbed him by the collar of his shirt, and away we went. I ran beside the bike, holding my son's head up while he pedaled furiously and wrestled with speed and gravity. Around and around the lot we raced, my grip on his collar gradually relenting. Finally, moments before I collapsed in a gasping heap, I let my son go, and he rode the wild machine on his own for a few eternal moments before crashing into a curb.

I raced to him. Unhurt, he gazed into my face with wonder and he spoke a single breathless word: "Dad!" He had done it, mastered gravity and momentum and pedals and sailed across the pavement.

I knew, watching him pick the bike up and prepare for another assault, that a moment never to be relived had just passed into memory. Miles of boyhood and teenage and adult bicycle rides lay ahead of him. He would ultimately explore the world about him seated above the wheels he had conquered today. But never again would he experience the sweet triumph won in this first exhilarating and terrifying ride. For this moment, like so many others, there is no encore.

Much of the history of love between a man and a woman is like my son's first ride on a bike. It can be savored and remembered, but never quite repeated. More than a few lovers may enter marriage confused on this point. They may imagine that their wedding vows commit them to sustain for a lifetime the heart-piercing infatuation of new high school sweethearts. The novelist Thomas Hardy cynically described this kind of unrealistic vow in his novel *Jude the Obscure:*

> [T]he two swore that at every other time of their lives till death took
> them, they would assuredly believe, feel, and desire precisely as

they believed, felt and desired during the few preceding weeks. What was as remarkable as the undertaking itself was the fact that nobody seemed at all surprised at what they swore.[3]

Hardy exaggerated the unreasonableness of the wedding vow. But at least for some lovers, he may have been fairly close to the mark of what they actually imagined they were doing when they promised undying love. If this is what the marriage vow demands of us, then we are doomed to fail.

The pledge of a lifetime love does not commit lovers to the impossible. A man and woman cannot always hope to repeat past romantic moments. But they can still build a romance that will follow them throughout a lifetime of a thousand new moments. Life does not stand still, nor do they. If lived as it is meant to be, life will be a bringer of new things, a discovery of new continents, an exploration of new vistas. *Eros* will feed off of this newness so long as a man and woman remain close enough to see it happening in each other's lives. If they drift apart and abandon intimacy with one another, then they will have nothing new to share and *eros* will die. But if they remain faithful to the labor of intimacy, they will grow and change together, and romance will survive.

Intimacy and Unfaithfulness

The labor of intimacy not only sustains *eros*, but it serves as a barrier to unfaithfulness. The great myth of cinema and paperback best-sellers is that unfaithfulness happens suddenly, inexplicably, that in a single instant a man or woman abandons the vow of fidelity because he or she is helpless to do otherwise. This is a myth, of course. Adultery seldom begins in a motel room. This is what Jesus meant in the Sermon on the Mount when He declared that when a man looks at a woman lustfully he commits adultery in his heart (Matt. 5:24). What ends in a bed invariably begins in a heart.

Adultery begins when a man or woman carves out a secret place in their heart to make an adulterous thought welcome there. At first this secret place may not even harbor the faithless thought. Only a secret dwells there—perhaps a conversation with a female coworker that the man knows would displease his wife, or a growing friendship with another man centered in things her husband does not understand or appreciate. But in this secret place unfaithfulness takes root and ultimately blossoms. Half-innocent glances are stored up there, conversations more intimate than appropriate, suggestive jokes. These secrets beget desire—hidden at first, of course, dreamed of but not spoken. This hidden desire may not inevitably yield outward infidelity. But if it does, no one should be surprised except the spouse who is betrayed. And even if hidden desire remains hidden, it will invariably steal the life from any love remaining between a husband and wife.

The labor of intimacy is the labor of preventing secret places from finding a place in our lives. It is the labor of assuring that no thought and no memory takes root in an unseen place, invisible to our lover's eye.

Part of my responsibility as a law professor involves talking with students about coursework, legal careers, and about law and law school in general. Although some of my conversations take place in the classrooms and halls of the law school, most of them occur in my office. I keep the door of my office open when I am talking with students. Every now and then a female student will enter my office, ask to speak with me about some matter, and shut my door before she takes a seat in front of my desk. I have never sensed anything forward in these attempts at privacy. Normally a student simply wants to talk about a bad grade on an exam and is embarrassed to have other people hear about it. But the first time this happened, I told Lee about it that evening. After I told her, we talked together about how I could satisfy my students' occasional need for privacy in our discussions without having the door to my office shut.

I will discuss in a later chapter the rules Lee and I set up to guard our love. Chief among these is the practice of avoiding close personal contact with people of the opposite sex. This means, for example, that I do not go to lunch alone with female students or even female colleagues on the faculty of the law school where I teach. I will discuss our reasons for this practice subsequently, but sometimes we can be caught off guard as we try to apply this practice. For instance, I play racquetball regularly at my school's gymnasium. Most games I play with a male colleague, and occasionally I play with male students. One day I arrived for a regular game and discovered that my colleague had invited a female student to play with us. I knew that Lee would view my playing racquetball with a female student, even when it was not one-on-one, as unwise. But I saw no gracious way of getting out of the game that day and so went ahead and played. I could have easily avoided telling Lee about the game, but the work of intimacy required that I share with her my quandary over this mostly trivial incident that night when I got home. In the end, we plotted together how I could avoid similar situations in the future.

I realize even as I write these words how antiquated they will seem to some readers. Our excessive caution will seem fanatical, perhaps, and at best, quaint. I will argue more in a later chapter why this caution is wise, but it is worth pointing out now that we have every reason to believe that lasting love is at risk in the society in which we find ourselves. The rules by which most of our contemporaries are playing give every appearance of being incapable of sustaining faithful love. If this is so, what choice have we but to change the rules, and change them radically?

The second comment that some readers may make about the simple illustrations I have offered concerning the labor of intimacy is that the secrets I have discussed have been quite trivial. And I suppose this is so. I have never had cause to tell Lee that another woman has confessed her love for me. This may well mean that Lee is the only woman who has ever found me loveable. Our love would be more secure if this were so. But it may also mean that our work of intimacy has never allowed a trivial secret to take root and become a love-stealing secret. The Father, who knows the secrets of our hearts, will know if our labor of intimacy has to some small degree helped to shield us from temptation, or whether He has simply seen that we have not been tempted beyond our measure.

Intimacy and the Locked Garden

The lover in Solomon's Song of Songs describes his beloved at one point with the following words:

> You are a garden locked up, my sister, my bride; you are a spring enclosed, a sealed fountain. Your plants are an orchard of pomegranates with choice fruits, with henna and nard, nard and saffron, calamus and cinnamon, with every kind of incense tree, with myrrh and aloes and all the finest spices (4:12–14).

These images of a garden locked up, a spring enclosed, and a sealed fountain probably suggest that the bride is chaste—a virgin. But they also seem to speak to a crucial aspect of intimacy: It is inevitably exclusive.

Lovers tell secrets to one another. They share hidden dreams and fears. They confess private longings. They are confidants. A secret that everyone knows, however, is no longer a secret. To be able to share a secret you must first keep it. To be intimate with a lover requires that you hold something back from others. It means that you must reserve a secluded part of yourself for your beloved—a garden locked up, a spring enclosed, a sealed fountain.

I don't mean to suggest that lovers can't have any close friends besides one another. But these kinds of friendships must be handled with care so that love's intimacy is not trampled under too many passing feet.

Lovers protect their intimacy mainly by seeing to it that they *are* intimate with one another. The heart hungers for intimacy, and the hunger not satisfied by a lover will tempt a heart to seek intimacy elsewhere. But even lovers who share a rich intimacy with one another can jeopardize that intimacy by how they conduct themselves with others. They can do so in at least two ways.

First, they can betray intimacy by betraying secrets meant to be shared only by the lovers themselves. Wise lovers will learn to guard their tongues against betraying secrets.

- Secrets involving the lovers' physical intimacy.
- Secret faults confessed by one lover to another.
- Secret dreams or ambitions that one lover feels comfortable sharing only with his or her mate.
- *Any* secret shared by one lover to another with the expectation that the secret will be kept.

If you wish to sabotage marital intimacy, you need only betray secrets such as these. Tell an office companion about your spouse's sexual preferences, for example. Reveal at a crowded party the secret sin your lover lately confessed to you in an intimate moment. If, on the other hand, you realize that the intimacy you share with your wife or husband is one of love's chief places of abode, you will guard your tongue as if it were an unruly child in a shop of expensive knick-knacks. "A gossip betrays a confidence, but a trustworthy man keeps a secret" (Prov. 11:13).

Second, lovers can betray love's intimacy by failing to tell one another secrets that they have shared with others. One spouse, for instance, may stop telling the other crucial happenings at work, while daily discussing these matters intimately with a colleague. A woman may find herself increasingly exasperated by some habit of her husband's, and rather than talking with him about this matter, may instead confide in a friend her growing aggravation. In both cases, love's intimacy suffers when competing intimacies rob it.

We will reserve for another chapter the discussion of how lovers guard their love from infidelity. But it is worth mentioning here how dangerous it is for a husband to develop an intimate relationship with a woman other than his wife, or for a wife to find intimacy with a man other than her husband. Intimacy is the incubator of love, whether the lawful love of a married couple or the illicit love of the adulterous relationship. Quiet lunches, soulful talks, late dinners, long walks— these are the diet that nurtures intimacy and thus nurtures love. Lovers who guard their love will stand on guard against the intimacy that develops almost innocently, but ends as a deadly threat to love.

---

1. Ralph Waldo Emerson, "Gifts," in *Essays and Lectures* (Library of America, 1983), 536.
2. C. S. Lewis, *Letters to Malcolm* (San Diego: Harcourt, Brace, and Co., 1963), 27.
3. Thomas Hardy, *Jude the Obscure* (New York: Everyman, 1985), 66–67.

5

Cushioning Love:
Acceptance and Courtesy

*M*arriage is a joining together, for better or worse, of separate lives. No matter how deeply a man and woman love one another, this joining together seldom happens smoothly.

Anyone who has ever built something from a kit knows how pieces that are supposed to fit neatly together never quite seem to do so. Edges don't match up precisely. Square pegs fail to slip into the round holes prepared for them. The picture on the box seldom tells the whole story.

Marriage is something like this. Lovers murmur before the wedding how they were made for one another. But afterwards, they may suspect that someone has gotten the wrong pieces mixed together.

It's natural for lovers to feel this way. Some tension is to be expected between two people learning to live together for the first time. Separate ways of living merge together at a hundred trivial points as lovers decide when to get up, when to eat, what to eat, what to do on Saturdays, what music to listen to. For partners who have lived for a while alone, the mere presence of another body around the house can take some getting used to. "Are you still here?" is the unconscious question of more than one new bride and groom. But lovers shouldn't despair. This first strangeness passes soon enough and should seldom amount to any real threat to love.

But even after lovers survive the jarring and hammering of their initial joining together as husband and wife, they still have to endure the ordinary aggravations of living with one another over a lifetime. They differ in important ways, and always will differ. Their differences often collide. Wants, needs, hopes, desires, and fears clash, a constant bumping and jarring. Lovers must survive these collisions. Sometimes things break, and someone has to pick up the pieces.

What lovers desperately need is something to smooth over the rough spots of their ill-fitting edges. They need something to cushion the everyday shocks of living together. They must work not only at sustaining intimacy but at simply getting along. They need cushions to soften the blows that they will invariably inflict on one another and that life will inflict on them both. In this chapter we consider two kinds of work needed to cushion love: the labor of acceptance and the labor of courtesy.

Acceptance

Eros embraces what it does not fully see. No wonder it chiefly inhabits the night, when sight gives way to the touch of lovers. *Eros* rushes forward to promise love and eternal faithfulness in the enchanted darkness of romance. It seldom stops to ponder what the day's light will disclose about a lover. The day inevitably brings its share of surprises.

It is the rare man and woman who, recently married, do not wake and move about a house in the early days of a marriage at least partially as strangers. *Who is this slovenly beast?* the most adoring bride may ask of a husband. *Who is this pale specter of a woman?* a husband may think of a feminine face not yet clothed with makeup. *Eros* cloaks in poetry all the sharp, prickly details of reality. *Eros*, though, can seldom keep up the game for long. After the wedding these details grow suddenly visible. The lovers' Camelot always looks less magical by day, more like a stony fortress with bad plumbing.

What are the suddenly clear-seeing lovers to do?

In some cases, the disenchantment produced by the early days of marriage may produce lasting resentment. One or both of the lovers feels cheated, as though a spouse had been lured to the altar expecting to acquire a near perfect mate, only to have an inferior copy substituted at the last minute. "You misled me" may become the unspoken accusation. "I want a refund or an exchange."

More commonly, though, lovers take love's disenchantment in stride. Love is a little blind, and deep down, lover's know this even when they are blinded by love. They won't seriously imagine walking away from marriage or a spouse who proves to have—well—unexpected features. Instead, they simply set about recapturing Camelot. They attempt to remake one another into the image that paraded out of the church under a shower of rice but was lost shortly thereafter.

Is he more brutish than she imagined possible? Then she will teach him cleanliness and neatness. Shoes go here, dirty laundry here. "Can't you keep your razor in the medicine cabinet rather than on the sink?"

Is she forever tardy? Then he will buy her a watch and school her in its use. "Always leave ten minutes before you think you need to," he instructs her. "Give yourself extra time."

Does he seem often depressed? Then she will rescue him with animated conversation. "How was your day?" "Is your boss still being disagreeable?" "Why don't we talk about where we want to be with our lives in ten years."

Are her interests and enthusiasms trite? Then he will rebuke her levity and encourage her to pursue more weighty matters. Maybe she should start reading the *Wall Street Journal* instead of a women's magazine. Maybe he should watch that remake of *Cyrano* rather than *Rocky III*.

The lovers will attempt to redecorate one another. The same hands that grasp furniture and knickknacks, pulling them into the form of a pleasing home, grasp and tug one other. *This* should be here, and *that* tucked into a closet, far in the back. A little recovering, a new finish, perhaps some paint. A minor adjustment here, some radical tinkering there. What parents and teachers and friends and even God have not accomplished, newly mated spouses will undertake without a shadow of trepidation.

They will almost certainly fail. This is reason enough to proceed cautiously. Men and women come to marriage with fairly rigid characters. The only changes in these characters likely to occur, especially in a short space of time, are those that begin inwardly, fired by divine grace. Nagging and threats and other external pesterings do little more than chip off a piece of hardened character here and there, leaving its essential form unchanged and causing nothing but sharp conflict. Redecorating a house is one thing. Redecorating a person is an altogether different thing, and one at which only God excels. When we set out to remake one another (usually in our own image), we are really pretending to be little gods. And since we aren't gods, we invariably bungle the job.

But the effort to be miniature gods to one another accomplishes more harm than simple failure. This effort also denies lasting love one of its most important foundations and its chief mooring: acceptance.

Listen again to the words of the traditional marriage vow. "I take thee to be my lawful wedded husband," she says. "I take thee to be my lawful wedded wife," he repeats. These words are not an empty ritual or a quaint relic of the past. They are the very charter of love itself. *I take thee.* Not someone else, not some creation of fantasy, not who I hope you are. *I take thee.* You, here and now, as you are and as you will by the Father's grace become. *I take thee.* Without qualification or reservation. *I take thee.*

It isn't really true that a good marriage is "one made between a blind wife and a deaf husband."[1] Acceptance is the eyes-wide-open taking of wife to husband and husband to wife.

Acceptance is love's resting place. The present out of which the hoped for future has its birth. A rock and a foundation upon which all else will be constructed.

In George Eliot's novel *Middlemarch,* a young woman named Dorothea marries an older clergyman. He looks at her mainly as a pupil to be taught or an unfinished work of art to be completed. "She," Eliot writes, "was always trying to be what her husband wished, and never able to repose in his delight in what she was."[2] The acceptance reflected in our taking of one another is a kind of repose that love itself requires to grow. It is the rest that strengthens lovers to do the work of love. Acceptance is love's Sabbath.

God Himself makes the repose of acceptance the beginning of His work and commands us to do the same. "Accept one another, then," Paul wrote to the church at Rome, "just as Christ accepted you, in order to bring praise to God" (15:7). Acceptance is the work of those who are spectators of divine artistry. The acceptance of love welcomes the Lord's handiwork, delighting in what God has done and is doing. It steps out of the way, patient before a God who doesn't need someone to pick up after Him.

Acceptance and Difference

New lovers rarely pay much attention to their differences. Under the gaze of *eros* lovers tend to see only how alike they are. Over and over again they repeat, "You like this too!" *Eros* blankets them with such a sense of unity that they fail to see anything but what they have in common. They wonder at how much their tastes agree. They delight in the same food, the same music, the same books. They are vastly different from one another, of course, but *eros* shields new lovers from the harsh glare of these differences at first.

But *eros* can only keep up the game so long. Eventually lovers discover gritty differences that appear to mar the harmony of their union. Suddenly, the match made in heaven looks more like a wardrobe thrown together from the odds and ends of a bargain table. How could the lovers have ever imagined that they had anything in common? She is not really so fond of the outdoors as he had previously thought. His reading tastes are not quite so cultivated as they seemed. He prefers the crash of an ocean wave against his chest, she the sound of the tide receding from the comfortable vantage of a lounge chair. He thrives on solitude. She gravitates to party, club, and fellowship. The lovers have different perspectives about what it means to be on time, what it means to relax, and what it means to be supportive of one another.

These differences do not really threaten love. In fact, they are sources of a relationship's strength. But many lovers don't see this. What they see is someone different than themselves, and they tend to imagine that what is different is defective. The work of acceptance begins when lovers choose to see their differences as emblems of beauty and strength rather than as points of contention. To see differences in this way requires that lovers reject the tendency to view each other's differences as defects.

I discovered in the early days of my marriage to Lee that the two of us moved to the time of separate clocks, and mine was apparently set thirty minutes earlier than hers. I like to arrive fifteen minutes early to any event. I learned that Lee was comfortable with arriving at most events fifteen minutes late. When I first discovered this difference, I tried to prod Lee gently. "Come on, honey, we're going to be late," I would say, meaning, "Come on, honey, or we won't get to where we're going as early as I would like." Sometimes, these gentle nudges worked. Usually, however, they simply succeeded in seeing that we were only five minutes late for a scheduled event. If I let up for a moment, though, and trusted in Lee's own instincts of time, the five minutes would turn into fifteen.

Frequently, I adorned my punctual instincts with the mantle of virtue. *I* was responsible. *I* was considerate of others. *I* was organized. Lee, conversely, was irresponsible, inconsiderate, and disorganized.

The truth of the matter, though, was that I was (and am) compulsive about getting to places. I don't arrive early out of any consideration to others, but because I find it relaxing to have a few minutes to get my bearings before the start of anything, and because I am self-conscious and hate to make a scene (or what I consider a scene) by arriving late. Lee, on the other hand, finds nothing relaxing in being early and is far less self-conscious about being late. I am not right and she is not wrong. We are simply different.

Visitors to our home need only inspect our tapes and CDs to discover that marriage can often unite radically different people. Lee's tastes in music run to Keith Green and Aretha Franklin, mine to John Michael Talbot, Debussy, and Nat King Cole. The labor of acceptance begins when we admit that our musical tastes are emblems of what the poet Gerard Manley Hopkins called "pied beauty" in his poem of that name. God "fathers-forth," Hopkins wrote, "swift, slow; sweet, sour; adazzle, dim." The Creator showers the world with not just one color, but a multitude; not a single taste, but a banquet. Speckled or "pied" beauty is His favorite design.

In Lee and me, God "fathered-forth" two very different people. She is primarily a whirlwind of deeds; I am more often than not adrift in thought. Aretha tends to be a fine accompaniment to deeds, Debussy more suited to thought. God has gifted Lee primarily to act, me to think and labor to transform thought into words spoken or written. My idea of a great Saturday is to spend several hours relaxed in a chair on our porch with a good book. Lee's is to plant two dozen shrubs and wallpaper three rooms in the house.

Acceptance is the work of not refusing to admire what God has done and is doing to make each of us unique. To refuse difference is to refuse His handiwork.

The work of acceptance also requires that lovers learn to see their differences as sources of strength, rather than as a threat to the stability of their union. Jesus declared to His disciples that marriage is the event in which God made of two individuals one flesh, joining them together into a new creation (Matt. 19:4-6). Each lover brings to this union different skills and aptitudes, each indispensable to the health of the union that God has made of their separateness. It is not at all unusual for one of the lovers to look at life from the perspective of nearsightedness and the other, as though farsighted. One sees mainly the details of today, the other sees the prospects for tomorrow. Together these two forms of seeing combine to give a relationship the proper blend of sight that fruitful living requires. The two-become-one-flesh relationship would be poorer without these different ways of seeing.

At many different junctures, marriage creates a oneness that does not submerge important differences between a man and a woman, but celebrates them. Visionary and practical, spontaneous and reserved, playful and serious. These differences do not destroy a marriage. They make it richer, sturdier, and more enduring. So "incomparably better," C. S. Lewis suggested:

> It is of the very nature of the real that it should have sharp corners and rough edges, that it should be resistant, should be itself. Dream-furniture is the only kind on which you never stub your toes or bang your knee. You and I have both known happy marriage. But how different our wives were from the imaginary mistresses of our adolescent dreams! So much less exquisitely adapted to all our wishes; and for that very reason (among others) so incomparably better.[3]

Acceptance and Sin

Differences alone are enough to keep lovers busy at the work of acceptance. This work faces an additional challenge, however—a greater one, in fact. Lovers must learn to accept not only the reality of their differences but also the reality of their sin.

Sin, though it may not have dominion over us, is nevertheless a frequent houseguest for all of us. We are each marred by its abiding presence and dogged by its step. If only the sinless among us can cast the first stone, then we should all have to lay our rocks down and return home.

Of course, this is not the whole story for those who are followers of Christ. God's purpose is to transform us steadily into the image of Christ. God predestined us, Paul wrote to the Romans, "to be conformed to the likeness of his Son" (8:29). He desires to substitute the nature of Christ for our own willful and selfish natures and to produce the peaceable fruit of godliness where thistles had previously grown. This is an ongoing work, one to which He calls us each day. "We, who with unveiled faces all reflect the Lord's glory," Paul wrote in his

second letter to the Corinthians, "are being transformed into his likeness with ever-increasing glory, which comes from the Lord, who is
the Spirit" (3:18). So long as God's transforming work remains unfinished—and it will remain unfinished for all our lives—we must
reckon on one another's sin. We are none of us altogether pure, least
of all those who see no blemish when gazing at themselves in a mirror.

The labor of love in a marriage is
the labor of stepping over
one another's faults and sins.

It doesn't matter how magical your love affair is. There is no charm
that will keep sin away forever. Sooner or later (and inevitably sooner
than we expect), sin will dispel the magic of love: a burst of temper, a
spat of selfishness, the ugly visage of pride. No love is immune from
these.

But love, though not immune from the effects of sin, can nevertheless survive sin. It does so chiefly by facing up to one another's
sinfulness and choosing to keep doing the work of love in spite of sin.
Sometimes this work is not so hard. We can step around a flash of
temper or a moment of selfishness like we step around a child's toy
left lying in the middle of the floor. "Love covers a multitude of sins,"
the apostle Peter reminds us (1 Pet. 4:8). Much of the labor of love in
a marriage is the labor of stepping over one another's faults and sins.
The great German reformer Martin Luther said as much more than
four hundred years ago.

> It is impossible to keep peace between man and woman in family
> life if they do not condone and overlook each other's faults but
> watch everything to the smallest point. For who does not at times
> offend? Thus many things must be overlooked; very many things
> must be ignored that a peaceful relation may exist.[4]

But sometimes it isn't easy to keep on loving in spite of sin. Where
sin is hurtful or vicious or unrelenting, it isn't easy to hide. And love
comes hard then.

There isn't a simple formula for love in these hard cases, surely not one to be found in this book or any other marriage book. *Eros* and ordinary affection will wither before sin's hot blast. Only *agape* can triumph over sin, only *agape* born of divine grace—no substitutions, no inferior copies. To perform the labor of love in the face of such sin is the surest evidence that God's fruitful grace is operating within us. *Agape* keeps on loving in spite of sin, keeps on believing that love is worth the effort, keeps on hoping to see the fruit of God's transforming power in a spouse—and in ourselves.

Have husband and wife no other part, then, in the work of becoming that which all of us are called? Must we simply endure one another's sin? Certainly lovers will be laborers together with the Father in the work of prayer, lifting up each other's life to the Great Lover, waving one another's names before the Almighty like the Old Testament priests waved an offering before Jehovah. They should also function as reflections for each other of the Father's transforming grace. No nagging or rebuke can so quickly spur me on to submitting myself to the Lord's transforming work as the visible testimony of His work in Lee's life. Her devotion to Christ is frequently a pathway down which I am moved to follow Him more closely.

But beyond the work of acceptance and prayer and example, I doubt whether lovers are well-suited to undertake any more direct work at remolding one another into a better, or more holy, image. Nagging, criticism, and rebuke undermine the labor of acceptance. These attempts to reform our lovers jeopardize the repose that lovers are called to create for one another. They frequently rush ahead of God Himself, even when rightly directed.

Courtesy

Love's second cushioning labor is courtesy. Courtesy is the work of attending, in mostly minor matters, to the needs and feelings of others before our own. It does not require grand sacrifice—we reserve other words to speak of these kinds of sacrifices—but small deeds of kindness and grace. As Emily Dickinson wrote,

> By Chivalries as tiny,
>   A Blossom, or a Book,
> The seeds of smiles are planted —
>   Which blossom in the dark.

Courtesy speaks a pleasant word of greeting to a stranger, pours another's cup of coffee before our own, holds a door open for hands laden with packages, lets a car pull in from a side street as we creep along in a line of traffic. Courtesy consists of all those minor acts of grace that will never win a Nobel prize for peace but which soften with miniature kindnesses the hard edges of life. Whether practiced among strangers or friends, courtesy wages war against the pride and selfishness that make life intolerable.

We can fake courtesy, of course. People do it all the time. It's hard to pay sincere attention to the needs and feelings of others. Most of us are too self-absorbed to devote much real attention to any lives but our own. But we manage to fake it anyway. We rely on a variety of minor social rituals that disguise themselves as real courtesy: We ask about a colleague's children or hold a door open while others pass through first. Doing these things doesn't involve real courtesy because we aren't actually paying attention to others when we do them. We think about the day's problems or the possibility of a raise while we hold the door open for someone. We worry about unpaid bills while we ask an acquaintance about her family without listening for the reply. Formal courtesy requires only the asking, not the listening. Real courtesy requires both.

Now, righteous souls may complain that fake courtesy is just a polite form of hypocrisy by pretending to care about others when we don't really care. And perhaps fake courtesy is hypocritical. But I suspect that even hypocritical courtesy is better than blatant egoism and selfishness. I would almost always prefer to be seated on a plane beside a man who thinks a great deal of himself but has schooled himself in silence than beside one who both regards himself highly and attempts to persuade me to a similar regard.

Now the tragedy of many marriages is that husbands and wives have convinced themselves that courtesy—whether real or fake—is no more necessary to married life than a three-piece suit is to a summer picnic. George Eliot wrote of a character in *Middlemarch* that she "was accustomed to think that entire freedom from the necessity of behaving agreeably was included in the Almighty's intentions about families." This way of thinking is extraordinarily common. Not a few husbands and wives have decided that home is where people ought to be free to be "themselves." The selves uncaged at home are seldom very pretty. Free to be "one's self" becomes a license for those who say "please" to every bank teller or waiter to make curt demands of a lover, and for faces painted with a smile for half a hundred strangers encountered during the day to mutate into a perpetual scowl before the light of a television set. Free to be "one's self" all too often means nothing more than free to be rude and inconsiderate.

To proclaim one's self free of the requirements of real courtesy is to pronounce freedom from the obligation of love, since courtesy and its unselfish regard for others is a child of love. In fact, the labor of courtesy is one of love's most important labors. And lasting love requires real, rather than sham, courtesy.

"Character," Dwight L. Moody is reported to have said, "is what a man is in the dark." He could have said as well that character—including the virtue of courtesy—is what a man is when he takes off the clothes he wore to work or to church.

What does the labor of courtesy require of a husband and wife who have committed themselves to loving one another? In the first place, it requires a reorientation of the heart's regard from itself to the beloved. Love is not rude, the apostle Paul wrote in 1 Corinthians 13:5, and declared immediately after that love "is not self-seeking." Rudeness, the opposite pole from courtesy, is the child of selfishness. We must be clear at this point. Whatever a home is for, it is not intended as the refuge for a selfishness we are afraid will serve us ill at work or church but which we coddle and pamper at the expense of our spouse and children. If the "self" we seek freedom to be at home is a selfish one, we may as well declare the labor of love forever abandoned.

Courtesy, then, requires a turning of my heart toward my wife and her needs and feelings. In the second place, courtesy requires attention to mostly little things. It needs almost a downward gaze, a focus on the ordinary and mundane rather than the extraordinary and momentous. Courtesy has more in common with footwashing than martyrdom. It is more like giving a bouquet of wild flowers than an expensive pearl necklace. Many lovers stumble precisely at this point. They think that a life of toil at an office or in a kitchen crowded with children is a sacrifice sufficient to satisfy love's demand. But the work and the sacrifices of love take many forms: some great and noble, others more quiet and humble. Courtesy requires this latter kind of work and sacrifice. It is a car door opened, a cup of water volunteered, an ever so quiet singing of another's self rather than my own. You cannot look too high for the work of courtesy.

For those who have trouble imagining the kinds of work that courtesy involves, let me propose an exercise. Spend a few minutes recalling the little things that you did for your lover when you were first married, or—better yet—when you were first dating. Such things were probably courtesy's work. This work came naturally at first: Courtesy is one of the handmaidens of *eros*. Now courtesy must have the support of *agape*, the love of action and deed rather than mere passion.

Here is my own "to do" list for fulfilling the demands of courtesy.

1. Open doors, including car doors, for Lee.
2. When I get up before Lee, fix a cup of coffee for her and bring it to her bedside table when I wake her up.
3. Wake her always with a kiss rather than with light or noise.
4. When she complains of being hurt or tired, sympathize and stroke her face or massage her neck.
5. Help her with her coat at restaurants and assist her in being seated.
6. Don't wait for Lee to tend to our four-year-old when she cries at night. Get up first.
7. Don't always play music on the stereo that I enjoy. Put something on that she likes.

I could go on. In fact, I should go on. Courtesy requires it. It requires that I spend less time thinking about myself and more time thinking of her. These acts of acceptance and courtesy make the work of love go smoother.

1. Montaigne, "On Some Verses of Virgil," in *Essays*, III, 5.
2. George Eliot, *Middlemarch* (New York: Everyman, 1930), 41.
3. C. S. Lewis, *Letters to Malcom* (San Diego: Harcourt, Brace, and Co., 1963), 76.
4. *What Luther Says: An Anthology*, comp. Ewald M. Plass, Vol. 2 (Saint Louis: Concordia Publishing House, 1959), 905.

6

The Labor of Avoiding and Resolving Conflicts

Occasionally I hear about a husband and wife who never argue or fight. I'm always a little skeptical about these supposedly serene relationships. Deep down I suspect that marriages in which no one ever fights are those in which one side has badgered the other into silence.

My own experience has been, well, different.

Lee and I argue with one another. We fight. We sometimes raise our voices and sometimes treat each other to stony silences. Our words hurt one another sometimes. Of course, I'm not boasting about our fights. I mention them only to confess the reality through which God has shown us His mercy. Our love for one another survives in spite of occasional anger, argument, and aggravation. Conflicts come and go, but love and the labor we do in its name endure. In this chapter we examine ways to minimize fighting, both by avoiding such conflicts as we can and by resolving the ones we can not, or do not, avoid.

Avoiding Conflicts

Meeting Needs

When our four-year-old daughter, Amy, fusses after lunch, my wife and I don't have to wonder why. We know, because we know her, that

Amy cries and fusses about this time every day. Why? Because she needs a nap. When she doesn't get one or when it's late coming, she gets cranky.

Cranky people start fights. Cranky people keep fights going long after they should have sputtered and died. And even adults can get cranky when they don't get what they need. Oh, yes, grown-ups have needs. Part of love's labor is for lovers to give one another what each needs. In fact, sometimes only lovers can meet the needs of one another. It is part of love's mystery—and its majesty—that lovers should be dependent on one another in this way. Sometimes lovers do a poor job at meeting one another's needs because they imagine themselves to be mostly self-sufficient, without need, or at least without any needs except the most basic sort: food and shelter, perhaps. But the man or woman who claims to be self-sufficient and self-contained, who claims to be without needs, is in need of a mirror.

More than a few conflicts between a man and woman have their roots in failure to supply these needs. Need sharpens irritability and increases the sensitivity to hurt, like slapping a sunburn. A husband and wife who meet one another's varied needs will sidestep need-driven conflict.

What needs do lovers have of one another? The preceding chapters have discussed some of them. A husband and wife need romance and intimacy, acceptance and courtesy. They need to be listened to. But they also need other things, and I will mention a few of these here.

The Need to Possess. A constant refrain in the Song of Songs is the declaration made both by the lover and his beloved, "I am my beloved's and he [she] is mine" (2:16). This declaration expresses two important needs of lovers: the need of each lover to possess *and be possessed* by the other. Lee, for example, needs to know that she possesses me and that I am not possessed instead by a career or a hobby or friends or another lover. She needs to know that I belong to her. She will know this when she can see me make conscious choices that show that I am possessed by her rather than by something else. When I am possessed by her, I will make sacrifices for her. I may give up one career and find another that allows me to devote more attention to her. I will sometimes say "no" to friends and to my hobbies. I won't act like a martyr, of course. I won't sigh and mope around, because doing so would show that I am not really possessed by her but am simply putting on a fine tragic performance. What she needs to see instead is that I truly move to the rhythm of her wants and needs, that any sacrifice for her is not even really a sacrifice, because she is more important to me than anything.

The Need to Be Possessed. On the other hand, my beloved needs to know that she is mine, that I possess her as a man possesses a priceless treasure, caring for it and guarding it. She is, after all, precisely this: a treasure. "A wife of noble character who can find?" Solomon asked. "She is worth far more than rubies" (Prov. 31:10). He declared in another place that a man who finds a wife "finds what is good and receives favor from the Lord" (Prov. 18:22).

One way of showing that I possess Lee as one possesses a priceless treasure is to admire her as a treasure. Admiration is the very heart and soul of the language of love. For example, the lovers in Solomon's Song of Songs spend much of their time speaking to one another in admiring terms. Another way to demonstrate a loving possessiveness is to boast about your lover to others, just like you boast about your prized material possessions. "Give her the reward she has earned," Solomon instructed his son concerning the son's wife, "and let her works bring her praise at the city gate" (Prov. 31:31). I try to praise Lee regularly to my colleagues and friends. She deserves my praise because she is my most valuable possession, just as I am her most valuable possession. In fact, I recently had the opportunity to praise her to my old high school acquaintances. The organizers of my twentieth high school reunion asked reuniting graduates to reveal their most outstanding achievement. I didn't hesitate a second in responding that my greatest achievement was in having married Lee and having managed to hold on to her for nearly twenty years.

What else do we need from each other? Encouragement, support, consolation, prayer. We need from each other the love of a Song of Songs lover. We need physical intimacy, not just sex (although plenty of that), but playful touches, holding hands, kisses hello and goodbye and goodnight. None of these things are optional. We *need* them. We deprive one another of them at our peril. We threaten love itself when we leave these needs unfulfilled. And even if our love survives, we will almost certainly condemn our marriage to an ever-escalating round of fights when we fail to satisfy the needs of our lovers. The surest source of conflict in a marriage is to leave such needs unattended. The surest way of avoiding conflict is to labor diligently to give one another what we need.

Accommodating One Another

A few years ago my wife and I bought a house in Mississippi where I teach. We closed the sale on the first of August and immediately a disagreement between the two of us opened. I wanted to move from our rented house now, this minute, pronto. Lee wanted to put off moving until she could perform major cosmetic surgery on our new house. It seemed to me that moving was simply a matter of finding the first weekend when it was not raining, renting a U-Haul truck, hiring an extra hand or two to help us, and just moving. I hate transitions. I despise those unsettling periods between events when I am neither fully here nor fully there. Left to myself, I would have moved into our new house within a few days after we closed the sale. By doing so, I would have kept the transition to a minimum and have quickly gotten on with life in a new home.

Lee had scripted the moving drama differently. She cared less about moving into our new home quickly than she did about seeing that the new house would be as pleasant as possible when we arrived. For her, this meant an exhausting (and, frankly, impossible) list of painting and cleanup projects in the new house which she wanted to complete *before* we moved. To me, all these projects could be accomplished as readily, or nearly as readily, once we were moved in. But Lee didn't see the move this way. She had a deep need to make our new house into a certain kind of place before we arrived there.

Deep-seated inclinations in each of us were thus pitted against one another. I will confess that the days surrounding our move were not altogether smooth. We had some fights. I was caught in a twilight zone of expectancy while Lee puttered about a vacant house that was ours but had not yet become our new home. She raced to finish the projects she considered most crucial before we moved, aware of my impatience and trying not to stretch it too far.

We would have fought more, I think, had we not done just a little of one of love's important labors: We tried to accommodate one another. Neither of us could follow our natural inclinations to their fullest. Each had to serve the other by sacrificing part of our wishes and enduring what we would have preferred not to endure were we not under love's dominion. We compromised. We adjusted. We agreed that Lee would take two weeks to accomplish her impossible goals, while I labored in the evenings with her and anxiously bided the time until this grating period of neither here nor there was over. In the end, we, and our love, survived a major period of stress.

Confession and Forgiveness

We might as well be frank. Lovers sometimes wrong one another. Sometimes, even, they hurt each other. More than a few conflicts between lovers arise out of these wrongs and hurts. If we could somehow manage to undo a wrong and to heal a hurt, we might sidestep at least some of our conflicts. But how?

Love can be wrecked by words or by silence. It can fall wounded before an onslaught of harsh syllables or be rotted away by bitterness that seethes in secret, never uttering a sound. And so there is a time for speaking and a time for silence; wise lovers learn to know the difference.

A healthy love ought to be able to tolerate a good deal of the minor wounds and wrongs that two people who bump against one another regularly are likely to inflict on one another. But this natural resiliency ought not to be tested too severely. It should be reserved for those occasions when one lover has unknowingly hurt another. When the hurt is known, though, the lover who has caused the hurt speaks.

This speaking by the lover who has wounded a beloved is threefold. First, the lover who has wronged a mate *confesses* the wrong. To "confess" means literally to "say the same thing" as someone else. In the case of wrongs, the wrongdoer says of the wrong the same thing that the wrong-sufferer says. "I have hurt you. I have treated you unfairly or rudely or harshly." Truthfulness and accuracy are important at this point. Confession names the wrong and names it in the same way that the person who was wronged would name it. Thus, the lover who, in a fit of temper, shouts some abuse at a spouse does not confess the wrong by saying, "I'm sorry, I'm a little on edge." Abuse is not the same thing as edginess. Confession calls abuse, "abuse." It labels rudeness by that name. It acknowledges selfishness as just that. Real confession doesn't soft-pedal a wrong.

Precision in this business of confession is important because confession serves to identify wrongs that should not be repeated. A confession is like a sign set up over an open manhole cover to make sure people don't stumble into it accidentally. Confession says, "This was the wrong I did, the wrong I plan not to do again." When we fail to confess the real wrong, our lovers have no confidence that we have recognized the wrong and plan not to repeat it. In the same way, to say, "*If* I did anything wrong, please forgive me," is usually to cloud the truth. When we say "if," we suggest that we are not sure whether we have done wrong. Since the purpose of confession is to agree about a wrong done, this uncertainty spoils the confession. It is in most cases a refusal to speak the truth, which is simply that we have done wrong and know quite well that we have.

A second word must follow the word of confession. The lover who wrongs another says that he or she *is sorry* for the wrong. Sorrow is the sign that the heart has turned away from a wrong. It also shows that the one who wounds recognizes and feels the hurt experienced by the one who is wounded. Here, real sorrow is crucial. A great British conductor rehearsing Handel's *Messiah* once warned his choir, "When we sing 'All we like sheep, have gone astray,' might we please have a little more regret and a little less satisfaction?" Lovers trying to apologize should almost invariably strive for a maximum of regret and a minimum of satisfaction.

Confession, the truthful acknowledgment of a wrong, and sorrow, the heart's turning away from the wrong, make it possible for a spouse who has been wronged to trust the wrongdoer not to repeat the wrong. Without a basis for this trust, the wronged spouse may take defensive steps to prevent having the same wrong inflicted again. If I ignore Lee when she tells me something important and then fail to confess and demonstrate sorrow for this wrong, she may be less willing to speak to me about something important in the future. If Lee scoffs at some dream I share with her, I will probably be less inclined to share another. These kinds of defensive strategies will ultimately do great damage to love. It is crucial, then, for lovers to give one another grounds for a trust that does not need to rely on these defensive strategies for security.

Finally, the lover who has committed a wrong passes the torch of speech to the lover who has been wronged by asking a question, "Do you forgive me?"

We do not escape the past by forgetting, but by forgiving. We do not heal heart-wounds by pretending they do not ache but by forgiving the one who pierced us. This is because hurt is a separator, and separation—the great destroyer of love—cannot be undone by any amount of forgetting. Good sex or entertaining television are never adequate balms for wrongs suffered because sex or television can never do more than cause a momentary forgetting of hurt instead of a healing of the divide it creates. Forgiveness—not forgetting—is what we need.

A person wounded by another almost invariably draws back from this other who has caused hurt. The wounded one retreats, as if to say,

"Not again." Retreat plants a space between two hearts, a minor gulf perhaps, easily crossed over again, but a space nevertheless. Hurt is also, by its very nature, a private thing. "Each heart knows its own bitterness and no one else can share its joy," Proverbs 14:10 declares. Hurt is a secret that one heart knows but not another. This secrecy widens the gulf between two lovers. Forgiveness is the stern work of spanning the gulf that hurt plants between two lovers. It is the bridge between lives separated by the sting and the secrecy of hurt.

The work of forgiveness begins with honesty—honesty first about the forgiver. Hurt and anger may prompt us to say, "He [she] does not deserve this forgiveness." But which of us does? Which of us has clean hands? Which of us hasn't hurt and wounded and left bleeding the person we pledged to love for a lifetime? Our ability to forgive rises out of our own continual need for forgiveness. If we hoard forgiveness, then where shall we turn when we have to go begging for it ourselves? To forgive another, we must first be honest about ourselves.

The work of forgiveness is also honest about the wrong suffered. Anger has a way of exaggerating hurt. A slight becomes a devastating blow; carelessness is transformed into calculated cruelty. These exaggerations falsify hurt, and true forgiveness cannot spring from falsehood. Just as the person who commits a wrong is honest in the confession of that wrong, the person who forgives the wrong must practice the same honesty. The labor of forgiveness does not confuse carelessness with intentional wrongs. It does not mislead itself about how often a particular wrong has been suffered before. *Always* and *never* are severe condemnations—and seldom true. Does a beloved *always* humiliate her lover in public? *Always?* Really? Is a lover never concerned about his lover's needs? *Never?* Anger is a liar, and words like *always* and *never* spoken in anger are usually lies.

Forgiveness, then, looks honestly at the hurt to be forgiven, and it describes this hurt. The forgiver describes the wrong to be forgiven just as the wrongdoer confessed the wrong. This mutual speaking is the way that lovers make sure they are talking about the same thing when one confesses a wrong and the other forgives it. It is not unusual for lovers to misunderstand each other about hurts inflicted. He confesses his failure to buy an anniversary gift; she is hurt because she perceives his devotion to golf more intense than his devotion to her. He sees his wrong in terms of momentary neglect; she sees it as wrong priorities. These lovers may respectively confess and forgive, but they are talking past one another. Their words will not bridge the gap caused by hurt. The labor of confession and forgiveness serves to bring about agreement on the point of wrong.

"This was the thing you did which hurt me."

"*This?* Really? I'm sorry. I see now. Will you forgive me, not simply for forgetting a gift, but for forgetting you?"

The labor of forgiveness climaxes, though it does not end, in an act of will which puts aside anger towards, resentment of, and even memory of a wrong. Forgiving a wrong is like evicting a tenant if you are a landlord. It says to anger, resentment, and memory, "You can no longer stay here. There is no place for you." Forgiveness deprives wrong of a hook to hang from in the mind. It denies the memory of a wrong even a corner in which to stand. As we have seen, forgiveness does not begin with forgetting, but it ends there. It ends with a putting away of the very memory of wrong.

The labor of forgiveness at which lovers work models the forgiveness that God Himself grants.

> For as high as the heavens are above the earth,
>   so great is his love for those who fear him;
> as far as the east is from the west,
>   so far has he removed our transgressions from us (Ps. 103:11–12).

The psalmist refers to God removing our transgressions "from us," rather than "from Him." The image pictured here is one in which the transgressor is freed from the constant reminder of the transgression by God's gracious act. The Lord separates the transgression from the transgressor in order to banish the transgression but not the transgressor. We remain in His presence. Only our transgressions are removed.

The labor of forgiveness requires the same of lovers. Forgiveness requires that we put away the wrong from the lover who wronged us, so that he or she no longer appears before our eyes as a wrongdoer. "My husband who hurt me" is transformed into simply, "my husband." Forgiveness banishes the memory of hurt. It disconnects that memory from the husband so that he can stand before his wife's eyes again simply as husband rather than as the one who hurts.

Like a garden that needs regular weeding, the mind sometimes requires an ongoing work of forgiving forgetfulness. Anger once banished may return. Memories once dispossessed will seek renewed admittance. The labor of forgiveness requires a lover to greet each such return of anger or memory with the same inhospitableness. "You, again? I thought I turned you out. Well, there is no more room for you now than at the first moment when I forgave my lover."

The final work of forgiveness is a visible act that testifies that a heart has put away the wrong it has suffered. Lovers finally restore unity when the wrong-sufferer demonstrates *by act* the forgiveness that has been granted *by will*. For Lee and me, this culminating act of forgiveness is frequently a touch—a hand that finds another, fingers that lightly brush a cheek, or arms reached out to hold one another. Sometimes the act of forgiveness is an invitation to do something together, to sit and read side by side perhaps. These acts are the final signal that the work of confession and forgiveness have been accomplished in our lives and that the divide caused by hurt has been spanned.

Silence challenges love when it allows unforgiven hurt to ripen into love-destroying bitterness and resentment. Sometimes the only antidote to bitterness is speech that names a hurt and seeks to see it healed. On these occasions, love speaks. It says, "This thing you are doing [or have done] has hurt me deeply. I have tried to forget it or overlook it, but I can't. Can we talk about it?" Even when love speaks out of bitter hurt, it does so in language that bears the mark of love. It is the great foolishness of our age to imagine that speaking truthfully to one another is a license for saying whatever comes most readily to mind, however cruel and unloving.

But not every slight or aggravation or even hurt threatens to produce bitterness and resentment. For these more mundane slings and arrows that sometimes cloud our life together, silence is the surest way to bypass conflict. "A man's wisdom," Proverbs 19:11 says, "gives him patience; it is his glory to overlook an offense." Overlooking a wrong committed by a partner in love means exactly what it says: We *look over* the momentary wrong to the love that rises up behind it. When Lee, tired or anxious over some problem her day has encountered, responds to me sharply, I may choose either to focus indignation on this brief lapse in her normally pleasant temper and take offense or to look over and beyond the moment to more than twenty years of love. Love covers all wrongs, Solomon wrote in Proverbs 10:12. It covers a "multitude of sins," the apostle Peter instructed us in 1 Peter 4:8. Love looms over wrong and momentary sin and makes them seem trivial by comparison, a mouse scratching at the base of a mountain. A wise patience sees this love in a mate and quickly loses sight of a momentary wrong that becomes almost invisible in the shadow of love's brilliant light.

Truthful Anger

In spite of our best intentions, Lee and I, and all lovers, will fight and become angry. But we, and most lovers, can reduce the number of fights we experience by schooling our anger in truthfulness. Because lovers inevitably fail, wound, and neglect to fill one another's needs, conflict is inevitable in even the sturdiest of marriages. If dealt with truthfully, both anger and conflict can actually disclose problems in need of resolution between two lovers. But sometimes real wounds and hurts are hard to speak about truthfully. To do so may make us vulnerable to additional hurt as we expose the point of pain. It is therefore not unusual for a lover who is angry over some particular matter to vent that anger over another trivial matter that has no relation to the real issue. If this kind of sideways venting of anger is allowed free reign, lovers will find themselves caught up in silly quarrels over who knows what, piling one foolish dispute on another until the real source of anger is hopelessly buried and left to fester in secrecy, producing ever increasing warfare over ever more trivial disputes.

Truthfulness requires that lovers deal with anger and hurt honestly. If we fight, we must at least fight about real things rather than mere phantoms, trumped up grievances that steal attention from serious problems. This work of honesty—and it is hard work—needs to be undertaken both by the lover who is angry and by the lover to whom anger is directed. The angered lover must seek to explain truthfully the cause of anger—the hurt experienced or the neglect suffered. The person targeted with anger must attempt to pierce behind the sometimes sham justifications for anger given by an angry spouse and find anger's real source. Why is he or she really angry? Is this fight really about the insignificant thing we keep pointing to and shouting about, or does it express some deeper hurt or bitterness?

The work of truthfulness will probably not result in an immediate end to a conflict. The perspective of truth may in fact inflame a struggle by fueling it with deep-seated resentment or wounds now made visible. But at least lovers will be fighting about something real, and eyes focused on this reality, their ability to resolve a difference or heal a wound or redress a grievance is greater than if they continue to fight with shadows.

The War Against Self

Sometimes, conflict begins as the rubbing against one another of two different people whose differences are not sinful in themselves.

Part of wisdom is to recognize that not all differences in perspective or inclination are sinful. Different attitudes and perspectives frequently represent nothing more than the multifaceted beauty that is the Creator's handiwork. But we may as well be frank and admit that a good many of our marital battles originate in the sinfulness that dogs our tracks even after we undertake to follow Christ. My disputes with Lee more often than not spring from, or are at least fueled by, my irritability, my pride, my lack of love.

Marriage does not create selfish
people; it merely unclothes them.

Mostly we fight because we are selfish, because we are pleasers of ourselves, jealous guardians of first place for the "I" that would be master. We seldom battle over principles or in defense of the right and good. We grapple, rather, to be first, to have our needs satisfied first, for our preferences and inclinations to prevail over all others. There is no glory in this fighting. It is a scrubby, dirty, ugly competition of selves already enormous and seeking to be bigger. And no counseling or psychological trick can make these selfish wars anything other than what they are—a scandal to Christ and a betrayal of the work He seeks to accomplish within us.

The only real peace to be enforced against the conflict of selfishness is the peace of Christ won as we are transformed by God into the image of Christ. This is not a book about the long process of this transformation, by which the grasping and conniving self dies and a new creation in Christ's image supplants it. But this process of transformation, the only sure source of lasting love, will inevitably find its chief evidence in the prickly intimacy of marriage, where we bump and jostle against one another without all the superficial manners that disguise a selfish heart in public. "We are only what we always were, but naked now," one of the characters in Arthur Miller's play *The Crucible* declares.[1] Marriage does not create selfish people; it merely unclothes them. And the glory that we reflect as the Father transforms us into the image of Christ will illuminate our marriages, if it is to illuminate us at all. We are almost certainly deceiving ourselves about the measure of our faithfulness to Christ if our lovers who see us unclothed both physically and spiritually cannot see, however dimly, the costly treasure of Christ hidden in the earthly vessels of ourselves.

Resolving Conflicts

Love can weather conflict. Like a solid piece of furniture, it can withstand a fair amount of knocking about without breaking. This was one of Lee's early discoveries after we were married. At first, every petty squabble we had was for her a bell tolling the death of love. Each fight, no matter how minor, seemed like the beginning of the end to her. "This is it," she thought, "this is the moment when love begins to die." But our love didn't die. It shrugged off conflict like an outgrown coat. We went on loving, and Lee gradually came to trust its durability.

What love cannot weather, though, is all-out war or the corroding bitterness that some conflicts leave in their wake. The most fiery passion can be quenched by a siege of conflict or by a bitterness that eats away at the roots of love. These are the great enemies of lasting love. We must protect love against these at all cost. Healthy love can tolerate an occasional fight, but lovers must avoid war and must see that minor skirmishes do not dissolve into bitterness. For this, a man and a woman must learn to build a barricade around conflict so that it cannot expand into prolonged fighting or slink away as bitterness.

The necessary labor of love in the area of conflict requires lovers to build four walls around every fight; four walls keep a small fight small and see that it does not either expand into a conflict larger than they can easily handle or escape as a bitterness that can ultimately destroy the foundations of love. These four walls are four don'ts.

Don't Let the Sun Go Down on Your Wrath

Conflict is like a living organism. Generally, the bigger fights last longer. The best way to keep a fight manageable is to keep it small. And the best way to keep a small conflict from growing into a large one is to kill it before it has a chance to grow. Anger left unattended will normally die, and so Scripture commands us to see that the sun does not go down while we are still angry (Eph. 4:26). In other words, we are not to go on feeding anger into the night. We are not to give it a place to rest in our hearts until the morning.

The scriptural command seems hard, impossible even. We are prone to think that our emotions, including our anger, are beyond our control. How, then, do we control the uncontrollable?

Just as *agape*, the love of will and act, can create circumstances hospitable to *eros* and *sterge* and *phile*, so we can, by acts of our wills, create circumstances in which anger will find it hard to survive into the night.

Anger consumes emotional energy. It gets tired and runs out of steam if left to itself. Therefore, to see that anger doesn't survive from one day to the next, lovers must keep anger from gaining reinforcements. The chief way that anger can obtain emotional reinforcements is for a man and woman to separate from one another in anger. Although getting away from one another will sometimes allow anger to cool, it frequently will only buy anger a breathing space so that it can renew itself. Even when separation cools anger, it reinforces a dangerous pattern. It teaches a man and woman that what they cannot resolve together can be resolved if they leave one another. These minor separations thus engrain in the man and woman a habit of separation. For two people who are committed to forging a lasting love, the habit of separation is absolutely dangerous. Each minor separation is like a miniature dress-rehearsal for a final, love-shattering separation. What we practice, we become good at. If we don't wish to separate, we will be careful not to practice doing so.

By separating from one another in anger, a man and woman also deprive themselves of a powerful antidote to anger. If I leave Lee in anger, I will not see the hurt in her face that our fight has caused. I will not see her tears or her pain, nor will she see mine. I will carry away with me only the memory of the harsh words she might have spoken, the cold gaze she may have turned upon me. And with these memories, my anger may well renew itself. How dare she speak to me the way she did! How dare she look at me that way! These are the memories that will allow anger to feed on itself.

Anger, therefore, must be made to live with its consequences. Lee and I have practiced now for nearly twenty years several ways of making anger look into its own face.

First, we make it a hard and fast rule that neither of us can leave home and sleep somewhere else when we are angry. No one retreats to parents or to the sofas of friends. Second, we will not sleep in separate places, even within our own house. Sleeping on a couch or in a child's bed is forbidden when we are angry. By confining anger to the narrowness of our bed, we force ourselves to see its consequences up close, to feel its heat, and hear its icy silence. Third, we try not to mask the silence of anger with other sounds. The television stays off. There is no noise to cover up the stony silence of anger. Without a place to hide, anger hangs like a mist in the air. We cannot ignore it. It is like a filthy animal that has managed to sneak into the house, fouling the place where we live. Almost immediately we are looking for a way to get rid of it.

Each of these tactics assures that we will have to face up to our anger. We want to force ourselves to see that it is alien and strange. We want to make ourselves stare into the face of our wrath and shudder at its ugliness. Frequently, because we have tried to make ourselves sensitive to the unpleasantness of anger and because we have forced ourselves to face this unpleasantness, one or both of us will do something to put away our anger. This may mean apologizing for our part in the fight, either in causing it or in keeping it going. Often, however, neither of us is ready to apologize immediately. So we take a smaller step toward reconciliation—one of us simply reaches to touch the other. I come up behind Lee and hug her. Or she reaches out her hand and lays it on top of mine. In the language of our love, these touchings mean, "I'm not necessarily ready to sort through what caused this fight right now, but I want you to know that I still love you."

Sometimes we touch, and in a few minutes we try to talk more calmly about what roused our anger before. Sometimes we get angry again and have to start over. The hard silence. The realization that we don't like being angry with one another. The touching.

Occasionally none of this works, and we go to bed angry. Our final rule for putting away wrath comes into play at this point. We are in the same bed, you recall. Close enough to hear each other breath or sigh or weep. Now, before we fall to sleep in anger, we are both responsible for taking one last step to put away wrath. One of us must reach out a hand or an arm or a leg and touch the other. The one touched must respond with a like gesture. Nothing more is required: no apologies, no attempt to get to the bottom of what we were fighting about. Only a touch given and a touch returned. We force our bodies to display one small sign of love, and our hearts, more often than not, follow. Anger is put away, and we sleep.

Putting away anger before the day ends does not necessarily mean getting to the bottom of a conflict. In fact, at least for Lee and me, serious talk about why we got into a fight frequently happens hours after our anger has subsided, often the next day.

Our most memorable fight happened when Lee was pregnant with our first child. I did something to aggravate her—neither of us can remember now—and Lee decided to go for a drive in the car by herself. I insisted on going with her—she was, after all, pregnant and we lived outside of town—and what had been aggravation quickly turned into anger. Within a few minutes of driving we were bickering at full tilt. A few minutes later, still within a mile or so of our house, I seized on the bull-headed idea of stopping the car, leaving Lee to take her precious ride alone, and setting off on foot toward our house. Lee was now rightfully incensed. What had been bickering turned to shouting as she followed along beside me, insisting in very audible tones that I get myself back in the car. Still not without creative resources for making a substantial conflict into a larger one, I had one final stroke of arrogant brilliance: I crossed a barbed-wire fence and set off toward home across a field where Lee couldn't rage at me from the car.

When I arrived home thirty minutes later, I discovered that Lee had been there first and left again. Having goaded her into rage, I was not surprised to see the not so subtle evidence of it in my study.

Like a spy movie in which foreign agents have ransacked a room looking for microfilm, my study appeared to have been made a miniature battlefield. All the books and papers from my desk lay scattered across the floor, and my computer, an Apple Macintosh that was one of my chief pleasures in life, lay vanquished upon the carpet. But not broken. Lee admitted to me later that even in the fever of her anger she had paused before throwing a two thousand dollar computer onto the floor. Instead, she delicately dropped it from a height of about a foot. I am happy to announce that the computer survived.

While I was cleaning up the study, Lee had set out for her parents' house four hours away. She had stopped, though, within a few miles of our house. She thought to herself, "What would a marriage counselor tell me if I could talk to one right now?" She decided that a counselor would tell her to go home and work things out with me. So, after sitting for a while, she turned the car around and drove home.

I have bungled my way through more than a few moments of our marriage, blinded by pride and bent on having my own way. But that night, when I heard Lee's key turn in the lock, I did what she has ever since declared was the wisest thing I ever did. When she came through the door, I took her hand and said, simply, "Come on, sweetheart, let's go to bed." We undressed, climbed into bed, and held one another until we fell into the sleep of lovers wrapped like a blanket in their love. The next day we talked, each apologizing (I most profusely) for stubbornness and anger, each receiving forgiveness that turned the incident into a humorous anecdote rather than a threat to lasting love.

We never talked about the mock trashing of the computer until a week or so later when Lee returned from her doctor with news that her bouts with pregnant aggravation and anger were likely to get worse before they got better. "Does that mean," I responded thoughtfully, "that I should get a lock for the study?" Lee smiled, we laughed, and another brilliantly colored thread was woven into the tapestry of our love.

By taking steps to put away wrath before the end of the day, we keep conflict small and manageable. Limited in this way, conflict is like a small, petulant child: unpleasant and exasperating, but something two adults can handle. Above all else, we make sure that conflict is not given time to grow up into something too big for us to manage.

Don't Drag the Past or Future into the Present

The second barrier we erect around conflict is also one designed to keep it small and manageable. We take steps to confine conflict to this moment—to the present. To do so we have to labor against allowing either the past or the future to have a foothold in our present conflict. It is one thing to work out a conflict rooted in one particular moment. It is another thing—and a thing far more difficult—to resolve the grievances of a hundred yesterdays or the consequences of today for a hundred tomorrows.

It is probably hardest to bar the past from invading a present conflict. The past typically steals in through two words spoken in anger: "you always" or "you never." "You always ignore me when I'm trying to tell you something." "You never help me with the children." A conflict erected on the foundation of "you always" or "you never" has far more to deal with than one which centers around the present moment. "You're not listening to me." "You're not helping me with the children." Accusations from the present carry less emotional charge. Generally, a spouse can respond more readily to an accusation based in the present in a way that will turn aside prolonged anger. "I'm sorry, sweetheart, I wasn't listening. I was thinking about all the things I have to do tomorrow." "I'm sorry, darling, I know I haven't been much help with the children today. I'm tired, but I guess you're tired too."

An "always" or "never" accusation is far more likely to provoke an angry response and thus compound one person's anger with the other's. In the first place, "always" and "never" will provoke anger because these accusations are almost always false. Lee is frequently late, making me angry, but she is not *always* late. I am frequently cross, making her angry, but I am not *always* cross. If one of us charges the other with "always" being or doing this or that, the accused will naturally deny the accusation and often become angry at being unjustly charged. "That's not true," we think, and we respond to anger in a spouse with a dose of our own anger.

We become angry at the charge of "always" or "never" not only because it is an exaggeration and therefore untrue, but because it strikes at who we are. For Lee to accuse me of not listening to her at supper this evening is to accuse me of not *doing* something. For her to accuse me of *never* listening is to accuse me of *being* something: insensitive and self-centered. I can generally respond more appropriately to complaints about something I have *done* than to complaints about who I *am*. One is a minor rebuke, the other a dissatisfaction with me in a more fundamental and threatening sense.

Of course, we frequently get angry precisely because our spouse habitually, even if not always, does something that we find disagreeable. It's the past, combined with the present, that produces our anger. If we cannot consider the past, it's like we are being told simply to pretend that we are not angry. But we are.

So what are we to do when we are angry because a string of past moments leads up to the present moment? We cannot ignore the past, since the past is very much the source of our anger. What we can do, however, is to realize that the time to raise issues relating to our spouse's character or habits is not when we are angry. This is another way of saying that not much good ever comes out of anger, especially the reformation of our spouses. The only thing to be done with anger is to put it away. The source of our anger can almost never be addressed while we are angry. The best that we can hope for is to put away anger and then, at some later moment when we are calmer, to talk with our spouse about the thing that consistently makes us angry. We can't tackle the past on an angry stomach.

Just as the past can make a present conflict too big to handle, the future can swell it into such proportions that it will rage out of control. We can allow the future to inflate a present conflict by making threats about the future while we are angry.

Some threats about the future ought to be absolutely out of bounds for lovers. To threaten divorce or separation, for example, is to repudiate love and faithfulness. I will argue more at length in the next chapter that the word "divorce" ought to be permanently removed from the vocabularies of a husband and wife. It ought to be rejected as an option for resolving conflict. Moreover, what is not an option should not be spoken of as an option.

Other threats about the future may load a present conflict with more emotional weight than we can bear. For example, if Lee and I have a fight because I have been preoccupied and have not listened to her, she may be tempted to say in anger, "I guess I may as well stop trying to tell you anything that really matters to me." By this statement, she has pulled the weight of a possible future into what may well be a fairly minor conflict. The future she has painted is heavy with consequence. To say that she will cease talking to me about the things that matter most to her is to say that we will henceforth live without intimacy. It is to say that she will not be a partner in the labor of talking and listening upon which our intimacy draws its life. And, since the labor of intimacy is one of the core labors of love itself, Lee will have predicted the death of love.

How will I respond to this prediction of a future without love? Well, in the first place, I will probably recognize that she has spoken in anger and that she doesn't really mean what she has just said. I will also realize the seriousness of our present conflict in her eyes and may be quicker to admit my wrong in not listening to her. But something else will have been planted in our lives by her words. A doubt and a fear. Will she really do what she said? Will she stop talking to me? Will our love go the way of so many loves, into a silence in which it cannot survive? Before her words I may have been confident that no conflict could threaten our love. After her words, however, a grain of uncertainty has found its way into our relationship. What may then have started as a garden-variety conflict over a ordinary moment of failure and sin on my part may plant a more dangerous seed that will one day take root and grow into something far more destructive than the present conflict.

It may be that I have taken Lee's words more seriously than I should have. But words are important. Our marriage began with words spoken before an altar and witnesses, and those words were important. I should be able to distinguish between important words and words spoken merely in anger. And yet, because words are important, we must both teach ourselves to treat them as important and to speak only the truth, even when we are angry.

Don't Hurt to Gain a Present Advantage

Anger put aside before a day's end seldom leaves any permanent marks on a healthy love. But sometimes words may be spoken or acts taken in a conflict that inflict wounds that will outlast the conflict itself. Here lies the chief danger in anger—that it will leave something permanent in its wake.

Wounds received in a conflict may cause three very different responses in the person wounded. In the first place, a wound may become a source of pain that yields continued bouts of anger. Sometimes the wounded fight all the more fiercely because of their wounds. In the second place, a wound received in a conflict may produce pain that prompts withdrawal. Some sufferers retreat into solitude under the weight of their pain. Finally, a wound may become a seed of bitterness. Bitterness is a poison that seethes in silence, resenting the hand that delivered the wound, inwardly cataloguing the wrong done among others until it ultimately devours the roots of love.

Each possible consequence of wounds received in a conflict is harmful to love. Although love can survive an occasional bout of anger, it cannot survive the unremitting anger that some wounds produce. Nor can it ultimately survive the loss of intimacy caused when the wounded spouse retreats behind a wall of solitude to suffer in silence. Finally, love cannot survive the poison of bitterness which turns love into resentment and lovers into enemies.

Wounds, then, must be avoided, and when inflicted in spite of our best intentions, they must be treated. But how?

A husband and wife must first determine that they will not deliberately attempt to hurt one another in a fight. The temptation to do so is sometimes strong. Especially if I have the weaker side in an argument, I may be tempted to attack Lee in a way that will hurt her to gain the argumentative advantage. Lawyers have a favorite maxim. When the law is on your side, emphasize the law; when the facts are on your side, emphasize the facts; when neither the law nor the facts are on your side, pound the table. Saying something designed to hurt a spouse is a useful way of getting the upper hand in an argument, especially when you are in the wrong. It's like a lawyer pounding a table. You may stun your spouse into silence or simply sidetrack the argument.

The ultimate cost of this particular trick is too high, though. You may declare yourself winner of the argument, but winning or losing an argument is trivial compared to the wound you have caused. It will dog the steps of a relationship long after the shouting is done, after the perfunctory apology and kiss. Better to lose than to be stalked by bitterness or hurtful silence.

Lovers must make it their aim to banish from fights all the verbal weapons that wound. These will be different for every person, and a spouse generally knows better than anyone exactly the spot in a mate that will most readily cause pain. Lovers must learn never to aim at such spots. They will concede a fight or remain silent before they will launch the arrow that wounds.

Sometimes, however, we wound one another even when we do not intend to. Knowing the danger of untended hurts, we add one further barricade around conflict. It consists of a simple rule. When one of us sees that he or she has hurt the other, *the fight is over*. The arguing ceases. No further scrambling to get the better position, no other barbed challenges. The person who has caused the hurt immediately lays down weapons and seeks to become a healer.

To heal a hurt I must call it by its name and apologize for causing it. "I'm sorry, Lee, I shouldn't have said what I did and I see that I've hurt you." I must also wrap the wound in a tangible reassurance of my love. The very fact that I immediately lay aside the harsh words of conflict will be one testimony of my love. But this fact must be joined by words and acts of love. I will tell Lee how much I love her. I will hold her as a visible sign of my love.

All these immediate reactions on my part are necessary to remove the brand that hurting Lee marks me with. In colonial times, law-breakers and sinners were sometimes required to wear a mark as a visible sign of their offense. A burglar might be forced to wear a large "B" on his coat, a drunkard a "D," and an adulterer, like Hester in *The Scarlet Letter*, might have to wear a permanent letter "A."

I want to be branded in Lee's eyes as a lover. But by wounding her, it is as though another brand, a large letter "W"—the one who wounds—is sewn into my being in her eyes. Our love cannot survive this brand. Therefore, I must act immediately so that in her eyes I am lover again, and not "the one who wounds."

All this discussion of avoiding and healing wounds may sound strange in some ears. I'm sure there are marriages in which every conflict inflicts wounds upon one or both spouses. In these marriages lovers give their tongues free reign to cause whatever damage possible. Tongues become flamethrowers, scorching one another, "set on

fire by hell," as the apostle James wrote (3:6b). Wound-filled conflicts may be the norm in many marriages. But they are deadly, and it
is possible, in fact, crucial, to change the normal rules of conflict if
such wound-giving is customary. Lovers must learn that it is possible
to blow off steam without scalding one another.

Don't Undermine the Community of Memory

In *Habits of the Heart*, sociologist Robert Bellah and his coauthors
use the phrase, "community of memory," to describe a community of
individuals whose lives are bound together by the memories they
share.[2] The members of such a community share a common past, the
memory of which helps forge for them a common present and a common future. Although Scripture does not use this phrase, it is clear
that the Old and New Testaments center around two communities of
memory.

The Old Testament charts the history of the nation of Israel. Israel
was a community of those who passed down from generation to generation the memory of how God had brought their forbears out of
Egypt and into the land of Canaan with a mighty hand. God, in fact,
commanded this community to make the celebration of this memory
the central ritual of their lives through the celebration of the Passover.
He commanded the children of Israel to communicate the memory of
His faithfulness to their children and their children's children. "Only
be careful, and watch yourselves closely," Moses instructed the children of Israel, "so that you do not forget the things your eyes have
seen or let them slip from your heart as long as you live. Teach them
to your children and to their children after them" (Deut. 4:9). Through
the celebration and preservation of the memory of the Exodus from
Egypt and the conquest of Canaan, God sought to assure the Israelites
that both their present and their future were secure so long as they
remained faithful to Him.

The New Testament narrates the history of the Word that became
flesh and the community of His followers. This community—the
church—is also a community of memory. Its central celebration—the
Eucharist or Lord's Supper—is the celebration of a memory. "Do this
in remembrance of me," Jesus told the disciples gathered about Him
in the Upper Room (Luke 22:19). The Lord's Supper celebrates the
memory of how Christ offered Himself as the sacrifice for our sins
and bids us each to partake of the new covenant of His blood. By
celebrating this memory, we all recall the past that has made us

members together of one body and anticipate the future when Christ will return.

God, then, seems to be very much in the business of creating communities of memory. In fact, His joining together a man and woman is also the creation of what will ultimately be a community of memory. What binds a husband and wife together over the course of a life together? What gives them a reason to hope that their love will continue to prosper and follow them together down whatever paths God leads them? At least partially this: They are joined by the memories of their love for one another. These memories of love given and received will be an anchor for the present and a beacon lighting a course to the future.

How do I know that I can count on Lee's love today and tomorrow? Because she is the woman who has now loved me across twenty years. A thousand remembered moments link the separateness of our lives into a single chain. Lee is the girl I kissed on a train to Chicago when we were still teenagers, the woman who waded home with me through chest-deep water after our car was submerged during a flash-flood in Houston, the soon-to-be mother of our second child to whom I crooned "Misty" half a hundred times during the last hours of her labor.

A modern song about breaking up begins with the lines,

> Where do you start?
> How do you separate the present from the past?
> What do you do with all the things
> you thought would last, but didn't last?[3]

The answer to the song's question is that you *cannot* separate the present from the past. If you give up the things intended to last, you have nothing left. All lovers, except those just beginning to love, have no other present but the one they have built together upon the past.

Memories are important. Like Israel and the church, lovers who seek to craft a lasting community of love must constantly celebrate the memories of love. They should regularly talk about past loving, reenacting it whenever possible. Their conversations together should be filled with the words, "Do you remember when . . . ?" Shared memories are the cords that bind a man and woman together over a lifetime of years. They are the foundation of today's and tomorrow's love, the undergirding of trust and faithfulness.

The final barrier to be placed around a conflict is one to protect these shared memories from the violence of conflict. I find it helpful to think of this final barrier as a simple rule: *Never tamper with shared memories in anger*. Let me suggest an example to demonstrate how this rule can be broken and with what consequences.

Lee is an excellent cook. She loves to experiment with new recipes. Once she made blueberry soup for a first course at dinner. I, on the other hand, am fairly stodgy about food. I value familiarity over variety, especially when the familiar means beef, potatoes, corn, and field peas. This doesn't mean that I don't enjoy many of Lee's dinner adventures. After eighteen years of marriage, my list of familiar favorites contains a good many entries that were once only a gleam in Lee's culinary eye. And she knows this. She knows that I may complain at the sight of her experiments but frequently enjoy the taste of them. Memories of about-faces on my part and (Lee would add) of occasional magnificent failures on hers link our lives. We are partially knit together by them.

But suppose that one evening in a foul temper I criticize the new dish she sets before me. Imagine that she accuses me of ingratitude, that I respond, and that our meal becomes a gritty conflict. Normally such conflicts as these will not last as long as it takes the food to cool. I will confess my ingratitude in criticizing her labor, she will forgive me, and we will go on about the business of loving one another. But suppose that while I am still angry, I suddenly declare that I have never liked Lee's cooking, that even when I appeared to enjoy one of her new recipes, I was only pretending.

This declaration would be false, since I have in fact enjoyed many of Lee's kitchen experiments. But the real harm I have done is not speaking a falsehood. The real damage to love has occurred in relation to the community of memory that Lee and I have become over the years. In a single instant, I have destroyed part of the past that joins us together. By denying what we have been, I cast in doubt what we now are and what we may become. Of course, Lee and I have far more memories in common that just those involving the meals she has cooked over the years. But by casting one small set of those memories into uncertainty for her, I will cause her naturally to wonder about others. "How much of our past is still secure?" she may ask. "What else has he pretended?"

These are dangerous thoughts for me to provoke in Lee. It is dangerous to tamper with the past in anger. And so the final barrier we erect around conflict is one to protect the past from momentary anger, so that the present and the future of our love will remain secure. Never reconstruct the past in anger. Never pretend that the happiness of yesterday was just a sham. Never undermine memory's home.

The principles for controlling conflict I have suggested in this chapter may appear to require both too much and too little from a man and a woman. On the one hand, for some who have grown accustomed to no-holds-barred fighting, these principles may seem to ask for more restraint than is possible. I can only assure you that they do not. Lee and I are both quite quick tempered. She comes by this trait naturally. The practice of law, which called upon me to assert my clients' interest aggressively, gradually taught me to be combative. That readiness to fight it out still lingers in my character. Both of us stumbled on the principles of this chapter while we were still newly married, though now they have become established habits in our lives. We fight, but by restricting our fighting to a narrow space, conflicts pass quickly and do no damage to our love. If you have acquired more destructive habits in the way you fight, then you must break the hold of these habits on your life like any other bad habit. If you are a follower of Christ, then He promises His transforming grace for this task.

On the other hand, the principles stated in this chapter may seem to leave too much room for anger and pride and general selfishness. It may seem that by building a wall around conflict, we have left ourselves free to indulge the sinful nature so long as we stay within the ring we have established. I do not mean to condone this sinfulness. It is God's purpose to transform the followers of Christ into His image and to produce in us the fruit of righteousness. He is not ultimately satisfied with a partial transformation that leaves room for selfish and prideful anger, even if it is only a little room. He desires to carry on the work of sanctification until no corner of our lives remains untouched. But this is not a work done overnight. Until it is complete, it is as well that we establish some barriers that we will not cross, even in anger.

Restoring Lost Love

It may be that you have picked up this book and been painfully reminded of a love long deceased. You may wonder, how does one labor for a love that is dead? Let me end this chapter by speaking a few words to you.

It may not be possible to retrace the steps that led you from the time when love was something concrete and tangible to this—this sullen war of a relationship, where home is gut-wrenching conflict or cold silence and being in public together is a charade of stiff smiles. But there is a way back. There is a way to restore lost love.

The book of Revelation in the New Testament contains a vivid picture of lost love and a recipe for its reawakening. Although the love at issue is the love of a church for her Lord rather than of a man and woman for each other, those faced with the task of rebuilding married love may find guidance in words that Jesus speaks.

In Revelation 2:1–7, Jesus writes to the church in Ephesus, one that has followed Him faithfully over the years. According to the Lord's own appraisal, the church had persevered and suffered hardship for the cause of Christ without growing weary and forsaking their Lord. But Christ, the great lover of the souls of men, wanted more than faithful perseverance. He had called the church at Ephesus not simply to work hard and endure but to love. Somewhere along the way the church had lost the passionate love that had characterized her initial encounter with the risen Lord. So Christ followed praise for faithfulness with blame for coldness.

> Yet I hold this against you: You have forsaken your first love. Remember the height from which you have fallen! Repent and do the things you did at first (Rev. 2:5).

How does a heart recapture love? Jesus suggests a fourfold way back from unlove. The return consists of an acknowledgment, a remembrance, a repentance, and a re-beginning.

An Acknowledgment

For the church at Ephesus, the rekindling of lost love began with an acknowledgment of blame: *You have forsaken your first love.* The Ephesian Christians had forsaken love; it did not simply vanish inexplicably. Love was betrayed by lovers who stopped loving. So long as the betrayers blame the loss of love on fate or circumstance, they will never recognize their power and responsibility to call love back into existence.

The great English writer Samuel Johnson once described a poet who frequently brought suffering upon his own head but never acknowledged that he was to blame for his own misery.

> By imputing none of his miseries to himself, he continued to act upon the same principles, and to follow the same path; he was never made wiser by his sufferings, nor preserved by one misfortune from falling into another. He proceeded throughout his life to tread the same steps on the same circle; always applauding his past conduct, or at least forgetting it, to amuse himself with phantoms of happiness which were dancing before him; and willingly turned his eyes from the light of reason, when it would have discovered the illusion, and shown him, what he never wished to see, his real state.[4]

Former lovers who would begin the long trek back to love must begin by pointing the finger of blame directly at themselves. *They* turned away from love. No one "falls" out of love who has not first forsaken love. Love is not like walking along a path only to stumble suddenly upon a steep precipice into which strong lovers tumble accidentally. Love and unlove are separated not by a sharp drop but by a mostly gentle decline. To get from the height of love to the pit of unlove you must place one foot before the other, over and over again, through countless steps. To climb back up requires not a leap, but steady footsteps in the right direction. The restoration of love requires first that we admit to having turned away from love.

A Remembrance

"Remember the height from which you have fallen," Jesus instructed the Ephesian believers. The loss of love is partially a loss of memory, a kind of amnesia that turns a once-loved spouse into a stranger by severing the spouse from the tangle of memories that give love history and weight. Lovers, as we have seen, become a community of memory in which a shared past helps define the present and direct the future. They must labor conscientiously to protect and refurbish the memories of a loving past. Those seeking to resurrect love do so partially through remembering what love was like. "Do you remember when . . ." is love's catechism, and those who have forgotten love begin by relearning love's history.

Remember the height from which you have fallen. Begin, then, by re-acquiring the past, moment by moment. Over supper in a quiet restaurant or even around the dinner table at home, launch an archaeological expedition into the past. How was your love born? When did you first call it by name? What fears and anxieties and joys and epiphanies accompanied love's first singing? If you have pictures taken when love was still alive, handle them, and recreate their contexts.

Look backwards and upwards to the height from which you have fallen. Do this even if it causes you to despair of ever regaining what was lost. No one who would scale a great height does so without first gazing long at the far distant peak, who does not imagine the views possible from its vantage and breath the very air that hangs there. *Remember the height from which you have fallen.*

A Repentance

The third command Jesus addressed to the Church at Ephesus was to repent. Repentance is a word out of favor in a world slow to admit it has ever done wrong. The Greek word Jesus uses is *metanoia*, which suggests a changing of the mind and a reorientation of the heart's momentum in a new direction, contrary to an old. *Repent.* Turn, deliberately and decisively, and renounce the steps that led you from the great height of love.

A Re-Beginning

Do the things you did at first. You cannot simply summon *eros* again with a word. There is no magic wand to be waved or aphrodisiac to be consumed that will suddenly recreate romance once lost. You may have been carried aloft to the height of love by fairies the first time. But the penance of lovers who forsake love is to climb back, step by step, without the aid of love's enchantment.

How then? By doing the things you did when you first loved. If you came to your lover with flowers in hand in those early days, you must gather them again. If your pen spun out lines of poetry, you must discover rhyme and meter again.

Do the things you did at first. It will be harder than it was at first, because by forsaking love you have forsaken the turbulent energy of *eros*. But you can train your lips to speak the words you once uttered and your hands to bring the offerings they once gladly deposited at love's feet.

But will these determined acts of love restore the reality of love? I think this was Jesus' implicit promise to the church at Ephesus. I think it is also a promise to all those who, having forsaken their first loves, obediently acknowledge their betrayal, reconstruct the memories of love, and, turning, do the deeds of love again.

1. Arthur Miller, *The Crucible* (New York: Penguin Books, 1981), 81.
2. Robert N. Bellah, et al., *Habits of the Heart* (New York: Harper and Row, 1985), 152–55.
3. "Where Do You Start," lyrics by Alan and Marilyn Bergma, music by Johnny Mandel, in *Michael Feinstein: Isn't It Romantic* (Milwaukee: Hal Leonard Publishing Corp., 1989), 18.
4. Samuel Johnson, "An Account of the Life of Ms. Richard Savage," in *Samuel Johnson: Selected Writings*, ed. Patrick Cruttwell (Middlesex, England: Penguin Books, 1968), 90.

7

Guarding Love
from Selfishness

*I*n 1855 the American poet Walt Whitman published a volume of poems titled *Leaves of Grass*. The first poem began with a ringing declaration: "I celebrate myself and sing myself." Whitman called the poem, appropriately, "Song of Myself."

The song of self that Whitman celebrated is the cultural air you and I breath. It saturates the clothes we wear, drips from our conversations, tints our perspective. We have made a national pastime of surrendering ourselves to the great suction of self. Our virtues are self-love, self-absorption, self-potential, and self-expression. Whitman's song is a perpetual hit among us. It went gold and then platinum long ago and shows no signs of loosing its place in the charts. We dance to it, make love to it, and sing it in the shower.

We are all participants in a great national quest of self. We invest lifetimes in finding our selves, improving our selves, and expressing our selves. As the writer Annie Dillard put it, "I wonder if we do not waste most of our energy just by spending every waking minute saying hello to ourselves."[1]

This preoccupation with self was almost certainly present on the day of your marriage. You probably received gifts from relatives and friends—toasters and towels and china—but American culture left its own offering at your wedding celebration. Cleverly wrapped in the media tinsel of movies and commercials and paperback best-sellers, the song of self lay gleaming among all the other gifts.

You no doubt unwrapped it, sent a note of thanks, and set up house-keeping with this gift displayed prominently for all to see. Thereafter, to memories of wedding songs would be added a different melodic strain, sometimes quiet and unnoticed, other times blaring and de-manding: a singing and celebrating of self.

Marriage counselors frequently brand finances and children and in-laws as the principle sources of the conflicts that break up mar-riages. But I can't help suspecting that the real destroyer of love is seldom a person or an empty wallet. It is a way of thinking that makes each individual a little god, self-sufficient and self-absorbed. Most marriages fail because two people never learn to say "we" instead of "me." Marriages shatter because a man and woman don't know how to turn down the volume on the song of self.

Let's consider first, then, what the song of self will do to a mar-riage, and then how we can guard against its devastating effects.

Marriage and the Song of Self

The song of self has its own kind of golden rule, a perverse distor-tion of Jesus' command to "Do to others as you would have them do to you" (Luke 6:31). Here is the golden rule of self-singing: Look out for yourself, and everything else will work out OK.

There is something so obviously *selfish* about this rule that most people don't say it out loud very often. They may not even think it consciously. But the golden rule of the self-song controls a good many marriages because consciously or unconsciously, lovers have adopted the following maxims.

The Laws of Marriage According to the Self-Song

1. If you are happy, then your marriage partner will be happy. Therefore, you need to do things that make you happy even if they make your spouse miserable. In the long run, you'll both be happy if you each take charge of your own happiness.

2. The most important part of communication is expressing your-self. If you keep things bottled up inside, then ultimately you will be bitter or snap or do something else unhealthy for you and your marriage. So you have to express yourself. Moreover, you have to say what comes naturally, or else you're not being

honest. And if you're not being honest, you aren't really expressing yourself. If saying what comes naturally means being rude or insulting or insensitive, then so be it.

3. If you don't assert yourself, people—even lovers—will walk all over you. No one is going to look after you but you, so make sure you do it. Your marriage will probably end up a divorce statistic anyway. So leave yourself some options.

4. If a relationship, including a marriage, keeps you from achieving your self-potential, then you need to get out of that relationship, because there's nothing worse in life than failing to find yourself.

Before we rush to adopt these maxims to guide our marriages, perhaps we should explore their consequences.

The Trickle-Down Theory of Happiness

During the 1980s, many people believed that if government allowed the wealthy to make money without the burden of taxes and stringent business regulations, then the money they made and spent would gradually "trickle down" through the economy to less wealthy individuals. We can leave the economists to debate whether trickle-down economics, as it is called, really works. But the trickle-down theory has managed to escape from the narrow terrain of economics. It now effects the way a good many of us think about our lives. For example, many people think of happiness in trickle-down terms.

It's not surprising that Americans should be more than a little absorbed in the quest for happiness. Pursuing happiness is one of the pillars of our national life. The Declaration of Independence assures us that God Himself has granted to each individual the inalienable right to "life, liberty, and the pursuit of happiness." And because we are no stranger to Whitman's song of self, we tend to think of happiness in terms of how it affects each of us individually. What will make *me* happy? This, of course, is a ridiculously selfish question. And however selfish we really are, none of us is quite comfortable with trumpeting the fact too loudly. So we have concocted our own personal version of the trickle-down theory, one that explains how it can be all right to ignore everyone else and search after our own happiness. The trickle-down theory of happiness says simply that if I am happy, then the people around me will become sharers of my happiness and thus become happy themselves.

How convenient.

Here's how the trickle-down theory of happiness works. Even though a man may leave his wife to tend their children while he goes hunting almost every weekend and even though his wife bitterly resents being so abandoned, everything will work out in the long run, according to the trickle-down theory of happiness. Getting away like this makes the man happy. If he is happy, then his wife and children will be happy. They will enjoy seeing his happiness and he will treat them better, being happy himself. Presto! Everyone is happy.

As you can see, the trickle-down theory of happiness is a great justifier of spending all kinds of time or money doing things that please me but that do not please my wife or my children. Most workaholics believe in the trickle-down theory. Sure, they're away from home until late every night. But they're happy, and so their lovers and children will be happy.

The trickle-down theory of happiness does have a minor flaw, however. It is mostly false. Happiness is really not very much like rainwater gurgling merrily down a gutter. Far less of it than we think spills from one person onto another who simply has the good fortune to be standing close by. There may be a little truth to the theory, of course. I really am happy to some extent when my wife is happy. When she has just achieved some goal or won some praise or enjoyed some experience, part of her happiness radiates upon me. But the trickling effect of happiness is minimal since the things that make for one person's happiness may well be inconsistent with the things that make for a spouse or a family's happiness. Real *unhappiness* easily smoothers trickle-down *happiness*. If my wife's happiness required that she be away from home until late every night and on weekends, I haven't the slightest doubt that my unhappiness at her absence would altogether outweigh any slight happiness for her that might trickle my way.

When I was a trial lawyer, I could find a great deal of happiness in working on an important case for eighty or ninety hours a week. There was the competitive thrill of trying to win, the excitement of flying to New York or Chicago to take depositions, the camaraderie of working closely with people I liked. Although the work was hard, I enjoyed it and found happiness in it. I can tell you from experience, though, that very little of my happiness trickled over into Lee's life when I arrived home, smiling contentedly after a late supper talking legal strategy with other attorneys. Of course Lee was happy in part because I was happy. But as I continued to be out late finding happiness that she could only taste a trickle of, I was also depriving her of what she needed for solid, soul-filling happiness of her own. Chiefly, she needed my presence, not my surrogate happiness.

> If kind acts should always require good moods, then kindness would be an incredibly rare commodity.

Trickle-down defenders argue that people who are happy treat other people better, and these other people then find happiness in being treated well. A man, for example, who escapes regularly from his home on weekends for golf or fishing may claim that he is kinder to his wife and children after experiencing this relaxation. This claim, also, is partially true but mostly false. Kindness and an even temper probably come easier to people who are happy than to those who are overworked and stressed out. The man or woman who labors long at a stressful job may need time to relax, and relaxation may buy them some happiness. But the trickle-down claim often hides the more troubling assumption that I can't really be expected to treat my wife and children kindly and lovingly unless I am happy. This assumption, if adopted, becomes justification for all kinds of crankiness and meanness to those we love and should treat lovingly. I *don't* have to be happy to treat my wife with kindness and consideration. It's harder to do so, of course, when I'm unhappy. But it is possible and *absolutely necessary*. If kind acts should always require good moods, then kindness would be an incredibly rare commodity. Perhaps kindness is rare precisely because too many people have assumed that they had to be happy before they became responsible for demonstrating kindness.

The trickle-down theory, in any event, is mostly a fantasy dreamed by people caught up in their own private dreams of happiness. It is a pleasant camouflage for selfishness, but no one should be very much fooled by it. Sometimes what makes me happy will make other people happy as well. But more often than not, others become happy when I, for a brief moment, forget about my happiness and think of theirs.

Conversation As Therapy

You have witnessed the scene in a movie, or perhaps have been there yourself. A dignified looking man or woman sits in a comfortable leather chair taking notes with an expensive pen. A patient lies on a sofa and describes an image of childhood: an abusive father perhaps, or a neglectful mother. The patient speaks harshly to the psychologist at times, pouring out pent-up anger, but the professional listener never responds back in kind. The therapist simply keeps probing, coaxing the patient to put thoughts into words, encouraging the patient to express feelings of anguish or loneliness or anger, to curse or to cry.

Conversation with a therapist is mostly a one-way affair. The patient releases bottled-up feelings and memories. The therapist says little. There is really only one self on display during therapy sessions— the patient's.

The kind of one-way talk that goes on in therapy sessions, the open and frank expression of self that occurs there, has become a kind of cultural norm in America. A good many people imagine that normal communication is something like what happens in therapy. They believe that healthy conversation is mostly a matter of self-expression. I express myself and you express yourself. For these people, honesty is the single most important characteristic of conversation. Anything less than honesty, even when the honesty expresses itself brutally, is unhealthy. So say your say at all cost, they will tell you, even if it hurts. You'll be healthier for it.

For a husband and wife who practice this kind of communication, most conversation consists of taking turns practicing self-expression. Sometimes this mutual self-disclosure can be a pleasant affair, a journey of happy discoveries. But sometimes the selves disclosed are angry, bitter, jealous, or petty. Occasionally the selves unleashed through therapeutic conversation fling themselves immediately into a fight with one another, grappling for control. Sometimes self-expression is ugly and things are broken in the scuffle of self against self. We should not be surprised if many marriages fail to survive the ugliness and the brokenness.

Even when these kinds of conversations are not particularly ugly or mean in themselves, they are frequently useless. Each spouse launches words in the direction of the other, but neither bothers to listen to what the other has to say. Conversations like this resemble the letters that composer Franz Haydn and his wife sent one another. The couple didn't get along well, and Haydn liked to travel just so he could get away from his wife. One of Haydn's visitors noticed a stack of unopened letters on his desk, and Haydn explained, "They're from my wife. We write to each other monthly, but I do not open her letters and I am certain she doesn't open mine." Too often therapeutic conversation is a matter of sending little envelopes of words in the direction of a spouse and having others sent back in return, but never opening the envelopes to see what's being said.

The Clash of Self-Assertive Wills

The song of self is not written as a duet. You will find no two-part harmonies for it. Only one person can sing this song at a time, and if two people try to sing at once, the melodies clash.

Self-singing brings to marriage the perplexing problem of two wills that don't always want the same thing. When differences arise, whose self will prevail? Whose career will prosper? Whose friends maintained? Whose dreams fulfilled? Whose choices will win out over the other's?

Although the song of self creates the opportunity for these questions, it doesn't provide any real answer for them. Instead, it encourages a man and woman to hide the questions behind the appearance of an answer. For example, the song of self may prompt a husband or a wife to believe that the clash of their wills has been subdued when in reality the stronger has simply beaten the weaker into submission. The husband has dominated the wife. Or the wife has dominated the husband. Intoxication with the song of self may also lead two people into a fifty-fifty compromise, where lovers allow the husband's will to prevail fifty percent of the time and the wife's will the other fifty percent. Thus, instead of real unity between a man and a woman that encompasses one hundred percent of each, the song of self offers up a sham solution that tries to hold half persons together.

The clash of individual wills is all the more jarring because both man and woman believe that they can ultimately do without the other. The isolated self-singer believes that he or she can make it all right alone. Friends are useful or pleasant, but not ultimately necessary. A husband or wife may make life more convenient, but their loss would not cripple the self.

The Lonely Search for Self

The song of self prompts me to ask a legitimate question: Who am I? It would have me believe, however, that the question can be answered just in terms of *me*. Who am I all by myself, forgetting the people to whom I am responsible, joined, committed? Who am I in a vacuum, sterilized from contact with people and God? Who am I alone, cut off?

A few years after Walt Whitman wrote his poem, "Song of Myself," the great American essayist Ralph Waldo Emerson published perhaps the most well-known of his writings, the essay titled "Self Reliance." Listen to his description of success: "It is only as a man puts off all foreign support, and stands alone, that I see him to be strong and to prevail. He is weaker by every recruit to his banner. Is not a man better than a town?"[2] Today Emerson might paraphrase his original question. "Isn't a man better than a family?" he might ask. "Isn't a woman more valuable than a marriage?"

Because the song of self is really a song about the *bare* self, a man or woman captivated by its melody will be tempted to abandon relationships in the hope of finding this self. Thus, a man wakes up one morning beside a wife with whom he has slept for twenty years, with children racing up and down stairs, and asks "Who am I?" What he means is, "Who am I apart from this woman and these children?" As we shall see, the man's attempt to so limit the question will ultimately lead him to frustration. For now, though, he may truly believe that the only way he can find an answer is to abandon these relationships. He feels driven to strike out on his own—to discover himself again. Before he finishes his quest, he may well have destroyed the relationships that held the answer to his original question. He will almost certainly have tasted the bitter legacy of the self-song: loneliness.

I have discovered that the song of self is prone to raise its raucous voice in the face of emotional conflict. Some mornings I have left the house on the heels of a fight that exploded between Lee and me. I leave angry and alienated. I arrive at my office and turn to work in an effort to forget what has happened. But I can't forget. My mind and body are in a turmoil. My stomach churns. If I am honest with myself, I recognize immediately that no conflict is worth this severance from my wife. No position in an argument can substitute for simply being able to call her and say hello. The loneliness that prompted God to make Eve for Adam seeps back into my existence.

At this precise moment of turmoil I have two choices. On the one hand, I may recognize the turmoil as a kind of barometer to reality. I can treat my churning stomach and troubled mind as a testimony that I am part of a two-become-one-flesh relationship and will not be happy or satisfied until that relationship is healed. On the other hand, I can say to myself, "I don't need this pain. I don't need her."

The choice I make at this point will have long-lasting results. I may shortly go home. Lee and I may either forget or resolve our fight. But if I, while our conflict was still alive, repeated to myself, "I don't need her," something intangible will have taken root in my heart. If I succeed in convincing myself that I can really do without Lee, even for a moment, then that same conclusion will come all the easier the next time we quarrel, and the time after that. Perhaps this fight was a trivial affair, with little at stake. But I will have turned it into something deadly serious if I turn it into a lesson in self-reliance. "I don't need her." "I don't need her." "I don't need her." Each repetition hardens me. Each hastens the day when the final straw will be broken, and I will be willing to sever the relationship that God created.

The Lazy Self

We are all in trouble when we start thinking that the normal burdens of caring for and living with one another make intolerable demands upon us and require extraordinary sacrifices of us. So long as we take these burdens in stride, assuming them to be a kind of minimum prerequisite for responsible living, then we will shoulder them with little fuss. But once we start looking upon them as monstrous hardships, we will be inclined to leave them for sturdier souls to endure while we find something less arduous to attempt.

Precisely this shift in perception is going on all around us. The self has stood up and shouted its declaration of independence from the normal burdens of life, including the burdens involved in sustaining an enduring love. "I don't have to take this anymore, and I won't," the self proclaims. "I will not sacrifice my career for the toil of marriage or the labor of raising children. I will not surrender my hobbies for the sake of either my spouse or my children. I will not suffer a decline in the pleasures to which I am entitled."

The self that Americans have celebrated so long has finally shown itself to be *selfish*. And, like a two-year-old in a tantrum, the selfish self is busy making a mess of our lives and our loves. What did we expect?

The Biblical Response to the Self-Song in Marriage

What, then, does the Bible offer in response to the song of self? How does it solve the riddle of separate selves who inhabit a single house and share a single bed?

Some questions don't have answers because the questions themselves are confused. "What does *green* taste like?" a three-year-old asks, and we don't quite know how to answer. The words of the question make sense, but not the question itself.

Here's another question like the three-year-old's attempt to pin down the taste of green: "Who am I, *really?*" The asker of this question seldom wants to hear that he is a husband or a father. "No, no, no," the asker responds. "I know I have a wife and children, but who am I *really?*" He seeks the naked self, stripped of its roles, untied from its relationships. He doesn't want to hear of responsibilities or of roles to which he is committed.

He seeks, in fact, a twentieth-century phantom. According to biblical faith, self-singers looking for the *real* self are looking for an illusion. Life is fundamentally about relationships. Those in quest of the solitary self, the bare self, the self that, like Emerson, have put off all external supports, are looking for something that doesn't exist. And even if they ever found this naked self, they would have found something crippled, possibly something monstrous.

Reality is at its deepest level *relational*. According to the Bible, the cornerstone of my identity is the fact that I have been created by God. "The Lord God formed man," Genesis 2:7 announces. "It is he who made us, and we are his," Psalm 100:3 repeats. I will look in vain for some picture of myself that does not include the outstretched hand of God's creative power calling me into being. I was made by Him, to know Him, and to be known by Him. There is no "me" save the one He created. There is no canvas of my life whose colors and brush strokes do not disclose His presence. I may attempt to distance myself from Him, but by doing so I do not find myself. I cripple and mutilate the self that He created.

The Bible calls this attempt to run from the God who created me *sin*. Since we have all run, it declares that we all are sinners (Rom. 3:23). By this the Bible means simply that we have all attempted to escape from God's claim on our lives as Creator. "The one principle of hell," George MacDonald wrote, "is—I am my own!" We are all like sheep, the prophet Isaiah announced. We have all gone our own way (Isa. 53:1). We have all tried to change our names and deny that He is our Father. We have all tried to leave home and find our own apartment. We have all tried to find a secret self apart from Him. Even the best of us has betrayed Him, and this betrayal brands us all as sinners. The biblical revelation after the first two chapters of Genesis documents the steps by which man and woman, seeking to define identities for themselves, attempt to escape the Creator/created relationship. The essence of the temptation in the garden of Eden was to become like God (3:5), to leap out of the divinely instituted hierarchy of Creator and created and to become God's equal. Undoing the work of our betrayal required God to reestablish the relationship we repudiated. The New Testament teaches that God did this by sending His Son to find those who had lost themselves and lead them back to the Father they had rejected.

The Bible, then, is at its heart the story of a relationship created and rejected and restored between man and God. But the biblical focus on relationships extends beyond the relationship between God and solitary man. The second chapter of Genesis describes the loneliness of the original Adam and the gracious provision by God of a helper suitable for the man. God Himself announced that Adam's loneliness was not good and required the provision of a helper (2:18).

> So the LORD God caused the man to fall into a deep sleep; and while he was sleeping, he took one of the man's ribs and closed up the place with flesh. Then the LORD God made a woman from the rib he had taken out of the man, and he brought her to the man (Gen. 2:21–22).

God thrust a new relationship into Adam's existence and by doing so expanded the definition of Adam's identity. Now he was not only Adam, created by God, but also Adam, whose essential loneliness had been remedied by God's gracious provision of Eve.

Who am I, then? I cannot answer this question without naming names. Because I have placed my faith in Christ, I will answer, "I am a child of the Creator of heaven and earth whom I call *Abba*, or Father. Because I am married to a woman named Lee, I cannot understand my identity without speaking her name, for she and I are one flesh. I have a son called Benjamin—'son of my right hand'—and a beautiful daughter named Amy.'" Their names help to define me. There is no me, no secret self, that exists apart from these relationships. I am, of course, more than just a husband, more than just a father. But because reality cannot be split into compartments, any search by me for identity will of necessity include these relationships.

And so instead of turning away from relationships to find the secret me, I will embrace them all the more fully. I will not find myself by rejecting God but by understanding fully what it means to have been created by Him and for Him. I will not discover my hidden self by leaving my wife but by understanding more fully what it means to be a husband.

Resolving the Conflict of Wills

Individualism cannot resolve the conflict of individual wills because it does not understand that marriage is not simply the casual association of two individuals but the creation by God. "What God has joined together," Jesus said, "let man not separate" (Matt. 19:6). Marriage brings into existence a new thing. Instead of mere individual wills, we have a joining together not just figuratively but in reality.

The question, then, is not, "What are my wants and needs?" Instead, it is, "What are the wants and needs of this new relationship that includes one hundred percent of me and one hundred percent of you?" Both the man and the woman are now charged with a new responsibility: They are caretakers and guardians and tutors of the one-flesh relationship. Their wills are joined in one common enterprise.

Learning to Lean

The law of creation is this: I am not sufficient unto myself. I need. I want. I hunger and thirst. And I must look outside of myself for the satisfaction of all that is lacking in myself. I was made to know and love God. I am incomplete, lifeless, and a rag doll until I lay open my emptiness to Him and receive and enter into His love. I am alone without my wife. God described Adam without Eve as alone and said that this loneliness was not good. Adam needed a helper, and so do I. "In the Lord . . . woman is not independent of man, nor is man independent of woman" (1 Cor. 11:11).

Lee brings to our relationship much that I lack. She is outgoing and open while I am quiet and opaque. She is disciplined and organized as a testimony to my melancholic restlessness. My weaknesses are shored up by her strengths. Hers by mine. We need each other.

Marriage is a matter of singing in harmony, of two voices blending together to create a sound neither could produce alone. This harmony of separate voices is the essence of its calling and the source of its unique beauty. Marriage sets before a fragmented world the visible demonstration of wholeness. It declares an alternative to the song of self.

---

1. Annie Dillard, *Pilgrim at Tinker Creek* (New York: Bantam Books, 1974), 202.
2. Ralph Waldo Emerson, "Self Reliance," in *Essays and Lectures* (Library of America, 1983), 281–82.

8

Guarding Love
from Unfaithfulness

When I stood before a crowd of witnesses and pledged to love my soon-to-be wife, I was promising to perform the labor of love with her for a lifetime. As we have seen, *agape* love, the love of will and action, creates the circumstances in which *eros*, *phile*, and *sterge* will flourish. In vowing to love my wife, I promised to work conscientiously to sustain the romance of *eros*, the intimacy of *phile*, and the comfortable familiarity of *sterge*. With God's grace, I am capable of performing this work. The oath of love I made was not simply a lover's wishful thinking but the very practical promise to do that which I could do, if only I *would* do it.

For me to cease doing the work of love is, quite simply, to break a vow that is in my power to keep. It is to break faith and to repudiate what I have committed myself to do. It is a betrayal of my lover and my love. This betrayal is unfaithfulness, the unfaithfulness against which love must be guarded. Unfaithfulness may involve an affair with another man or woman. But it doesn't have to. It may be prompted by career ambitions or by sheer laziness. Anything that causes lovers to abandon the work of love causes them to be unfaithful.

We must not stumble at this point. For those who have vowed to love one another, there is no such thing as "falling" out of love. The labor of love is not like walking along some high place where the slightest gust of wind is likely to cast us down. It is more like working in a field, feet solidly planted, sometimes in the heat of the day, sometimes in the cool breeze of the evening. There is no danger of falling here, only the danger of giving up the work. We cannot defend love against the assault of unfaithfulness unless we forever put aside the fantasy that love is merely a state of mind over which we have no control. We can, George Eliot wrote in her novel *Middlemarch*, "set a watch over our affections and our constancy as we can over other treasures." *We can be faithful if we chose to be.*

Lovers can keep on loving, or they can cease doing the work of love. They can be faithful to the vow of love, or unfaithful. The love that a husband and wife undertake is not a love that comes and goes according to its own fickleness. Make no mistake. "It just didn't work out" is the excuse of lovers who *choose* to abandon the labor of love. It is the cloak behind which betrayal hides.

Guarding love from unfaithfulness is therefore one of love's chief labors. It requires specific tasks, the first of which is a matter of starting out in the right direction.

Intend to Love and Be Faithful

The first and principal defense against infidelity is simply *to chose to be faithful*. Faithfulness to a marriage partner is something like faithfulness to Christ. "Why are we not more devoted to Christ?" the eighteenth-century writer William Law asked in his book *A Serious Call to a Devout and Holy Life*. He answered this question bluntly:

> [I]f you will stop here and ask yourself why you are not so devoted as the primitive Christians, your own heart will tell you that it is neither through ignorance nor inability but purely because you never thoroughly intended it.[1]

Faithfulness is first and foremost a matter of the heart's intent. I do not know what you meant when you pledged to love your husband or wife until death's final parting. Perhaps you simply expressed a hope that love would continue. Perhaps you left open the possibility that love would one day vanish as suddenly as it first came upon you and that you would be released from the severe words of your vow. If these were your meanings, then your love stands defenseless against the assault of unfaithfulness. The labor of love is too arduous and too long to be completed by anyone who does not *intend* to see the work through to the end. Like those who would follow Christ devotedly, lovers who desire to sustain love over a lifetime must *intend* to do so.

"Let love and faithfulness never leave you; bind them around your neck, write them on the tablet of your heart," Solomon admonished his son (Prov. 3:3). You cannot guard what you do not steadfastly intend to protect. Right now, grasp hold of love and determine that you will not let it go. Bind it around your neck. Write it on the tablets of your heart. Etch it in stone—not paper—so that it cannot be erased. Envision every possible temptation to give up the work of love, and decide now that nothing—no person, no career, no sudden temptation, no unhappiness—will weaken your resolve to hold onto what you have vowed never to let go. Shakespeare expresses this in one of his sonnets.

> Love is not love
> Which alters when it alteration finds,
> Or bends with the remover to remove:
> O no! it is an ever-fixèd mark, . . .

If you fail to fix the mark of love, to plant its stake firmly within you heart, then you have not loved. A lifelong marriage requires nothing less than the unbending, unremovable mark of love. And so, before you take another step into the precarious future, you should stop now and make the labor of love a matter of your most resolute intent. This resolution is not all that love requires, but it is the foundation of everything else.

It would be foolish and arrogant to say of unfaithfulness, "I would not" or "I could not." These are words blind to the fierceness of our conflict, deaf to the rage of battle. Here are wise words, words to be spoken in pledge to those we have promised to love and to Him who guards our love, words supported by a petition for His grace: *I will not.*

Guard Your Heart

The Almighty reserved one of His most stinging rebukes for those who betray the oath of marriage. The rebuke is recorded in the final pages of the Old Testament where the prophet Malachi acts as God's spokesman.

Another thing you do: You flood the LORD's altar with tears. You weep and wail because he no longer pays attention to your offerings or accepts them with pleasure from your hands. You ask, "Why?" It is because the LORD is acting as the witness between you and the wife of your youth, because you have broken faith with her, though she is your partner, the wife of your marriage covenant. Has not the LORD made them one? In flesh and spirit they are his. And why one? Because he was seeking godly offspring. So guard yourself in your spirit, and do not break faith with the wife of your youth (2:13–15).

"Guard your spirit," the prophet demands. Why? Because unfaithfulness is mainly a matter of the heart. You cannot give unfaithfulness a place in your heart without it ultimately spilling out into your life. The betraying thought that rules a heart will eventually rule a life. "The good man," Jesus said, "brings forth good things out of the good stored up in his heart, and the evil man brings evil things out of the evil stored up in his heart. For out of the overflow of his heart his mouth speaks" (Luke 6:45). If we are to guard love, we will have to first guard our hearts, because our hearts are "the wellspring of life" (Prov. 4:23).

The work of guarding our hearts is a labor that occurs both internally and externally. We guard our hearts first by defending them from particular thoughts or emotions that will, if given a chance, gnaw at the foundation of faithfulness until it finally collapses into an unfaithful deed. We do not have room here to describe all the ideas or thoughts that can betray love. You need only turn on the television or read a novel or watch a movie or listen to a coworker to find all the advice you will ever need to plant and nurture a love-destroying pattern of thought.

One day, for example, you may see a passing commercial and think for a moment, "I deserve to be happier than I am." You may shake your head after a moment and go back to the business of living. If you do, you will probably be reminded that happiness is mostly a matter of choice, the fruit of a life lived rightly. But it may be that you nod quietly and bid this thought take up abode in your mind and heart: "I deserve to be happier." You repeat the thought after a fight with your spouse or when your children frustrate you. You make the thought a friend. You imagine changes to your life that might bring you the happiness you deserve. Perhaps you might find a more sensitive lover or one with more money to buy the things that would make you happier. You imagine a new life. From time to time you brand all this wishful thinking. They are only thoughts, you say, and so you continue to think them.

The thoughts that seem so imaginary when they occupy a mind with fancy are more real than you imagine. They accustom you to grow familiar with betrayal—to find in it a comfortable friend. "Ah, yes," you say to unfaithfulness, "come in, sit down. I will go about my business, but please feel welcome to stay for a while." The unfaithful thought, like an ugly friend, gradually becomes so familiar that its ugliness goes unnoticed. You smile at its coming.

The imaginary fancy gradually trains a man or woman to tolerate unfaithfulness. All that remains to transform a betraying thought into a betraying deed is the kind of trouble or temptation common to all of us—a period of stress, sudden sexual arousal, a fight with a spouse. Unfaithfulness, made a familiar friend in thought, easily becomes a reality. "I deserve to be happier." One day that thought finally nudges you over a line you had never expected to cross, even though you had frequently imagined crossing it.

The law of the harvest applies to thoughts as well as to deeds. If you plant and water and tend a thought that betrays love, then betrayal is the natural harvest you will reap.

The thought you would be hesitant to share with your lover, or the fantasy you can't describe, are almost certainly capable of destroying love if harbored long enough and caressed frequently enough. It is a pitiful blindness that fails to see how frequently the heart's secrets become the hand's deeds. Therefore, if you are serious about securing your love against the challenge of infidelity, banish every unfaithful thought and imagination from your mind.

Reject Divorce As an Option

For example, if you wish to build a love that does not dissolve in divorce, then *remove the word "divorce" from your vocabulary and from your thoughts*. Before Lee and I were married we decided that the word "divorce" would never be a part of the vocabulary of our relationship. We were both convinced that marriages fail today, in the vast majority of cases, because they are allowed to fail. We determined never to give our permission. We decided that we would never even joke about the possibility of divorcing one another. We would certainly never incorporate the possibility of divorce into an angry threat. We desired to leave the idea of divorce without a single hook to hang from in our minds. We wanted to lock ourselves into the room of marriage and throw away the key. No matter what happens in the room, we wanted to force ourselves to solve every crisis together. As long as there was a familiar door out of the room, one whose knob we have glanced at occasionally across the years, we feared that we would run from troubles that could have been solved if we had only been compelled to remain.

Lee and I expected problems to arise, and they have. But our list of possible solutions to these problems has always had a blank spot where many lovers place as a last resort, "divorce." Strangely enough, because divorce was never an option, our methods of dealing with conflict have always included the realization that we were in this together for life. And this realization makes all the difference. Once a husband and wife lock themselves into marriage as though it were a room with no exit, they tend to behave differently than if the door were wide open and either could leave if things got bad enough.

First, by locking ourselves into the room of marriage, we create a strong incentive to keep things "picked up." By this I mean that we do not let quarrels and hurts so pile up until married life becomes unbearable. It is one thing to make a mess out of a temporary hotel room that will be abandoned after a few days. It is quite another thing to trash a house where you must live the rest of your life—where litter has to be either endured or picked up, piece by piece, by the same hands that allowed it to be deposited there in the first place. A husband and wife who realize that they will have to live with a lifetime's accumulation of hurts inflicted upon one another will hesitate to hurt one another in the first place. Lovers who know they will have to straighten things after a fight will be less likely to lose control of their anger.

It *is* possible to wreck a marriage. It is possible to litter it with broken promises and the shards of pointed, cruel words, and to fill it with such violence and pain that it becomes uninhabitable—so trashed, in fact, that no one can imagine how it could be made liveable again. At this point, divorce will seem to be the only option left to the two lovers who have become warring enemies. But, at least today, divorce has probably been an option in the minds of the two lovers-become-enemies for a long time. Would they have allowed this awful wreckage to spoil their love had they known that they would have to live with that wreckage for the rest of their lives? I suppose that there are violent people who will destroy whatever they lay hands upon, even if they have to sit perpetually among the breakage. But surely there are many ordinary men and women who only gradually destroy a marriage, thinking all the time that they can always leave if things become too intolerable. This very escape will be a severe temptation to sit idly by while a relationship gradually *becomes* intolerable. By locking ourselves into the room of marriage we discourage the tendency to tolerate the gradual trashing of love.

Second, we encourage ourselves to look harder for solutions to our marriage problems. Suppose, for example, that the health of our marriage depends on some extraordinary effort to conquer a destructive habit or weakness of character. Will we undertake this effort? Will we learn to control our temper or our sexual desires or our sloppiness? Probably not, if we are willing to consider divorce as a possible solution to marital trouble. All of us are prone to take the path of least resistance whenever possible. We are all inclined to sacrifice only so much of self as the moment absolutely requires. So long as divorce appears among the list of solutions to a broken marriage, it may seem a more desirable option than some radical self-surgery. But once divorce is removed from the list, we may finally see that some sacrifice of self is the only way to secure a happy marriage.

As long as divorce is an option, we will be tempted to call problems "unsolvable" that could be solved if only we labored more diligently at a solution. Trouble, as the book of Job declares, is a given. Man and woman are born to it "as surely as sparks fly upwards" (Job 5:7). Two people who live in intimate and continual contact with one another will not always coexist in perfect harmony. From petty aggravations about the character flaws of a spouse, to financial crises, to difficulties with children, trouble collects around us all like bees to honey. Love does not survive by escaping trouble. It survives by conquering or enduring it. But the possibility of divorce is seducing more and more lovers to settle for defeat at the hands of trouble.

It is a common fallacy to imagine that our generation alone has been assaulted with great trouble. However "good" the "good old days" appear, they were surely accompanied by troubles of their own. The rising divorce rate cannot be placed entirely on the back of increasing troubles, although we are all beginning to eat the bitter fruit of troubles at least partially caused by rising divorce rates. An earlier generation, however, was conditioned to view divorce as the alternative of final, desperate resort, and married couples were compelled to cope (or not cope) with the inevitable troubles of life from within the framework of marriage. That conditioning has steadily eroded. Divorce is now an acceptable social alternative to marital permanence and ranks lower among the list of evils that marriage may spawn. The last resort is now well away from the bottom of the list, and evils perceived as more grim have taken its place in our catalogues of evil.

For example, American culture tends to treat loss of personal identity—loss of freedom to be "me," whatever that means—as a blacker demon than marital breakup. Our generation cries out for the right of the individual to stand in the spotlight alone. This craving for illumination of the pure, raw self is an enduring legacy of American individualism, as we have seen. Over the past fifty years or so, this craving has assaulted and captured the citadel of marriage. Now the husband who feels trapped by everyday responsibilities as a husband and father will find a crowd of approving spectators who will support his search for selfhood in the arms of a woman (other than his wife) who will hold him "just for who he is." The couple who consign their children to a day-care center and set out to find self-worth and the money to buy stereos and clothes may be assured of hearty applause for having chosen what we collectively value most—independence and a sense of "self" worth. If independence and self-fulfillment cannot be had in marriage, then a thousand clamoring voices will be quick to assure us that divorce is a lesser evil than to be deprived of self-fulfillment. When the pursuit of self proves to be inconsistent with the work of love, no one should be surprised that marriages flounder and that divorce—the lesser of two evils—finds new backers.

The way back to the possibility of lasting love lies in naming divorce again as the great evil that it is and by repudiating the quixotic tilting after self-fulfillment that makes fools and traitors out of grown-ups who should know better. Hear the Almighty declare again, "I hate divorce" (Mal. 2:16). Shall we listen to Him, or shall we fasten attention on talk show hosts and their guests? Shall we escape into reveries of how much better our lives would be without this man, this woman? Or shall we merely open our eyes and see the bleak wreckage that divorce has invariably left in the lives of those it has seduced?

Making Love a Public Testimony

The labor of guarding love requires not only that we control our thoughts but that we govern our conduct. Love's protection requires concrete actions to protect against the temptation of infidelity. The first defense against unfaithfulness is the public testimony of love itself.

In whatever secret places love may have its birth, the work of lasting love ultimately declares itself publicly. The announcement of engagement and the public covenanting of a marriage ceremony are only the first testimonies of lasting love. Even after these initial declarations, love is guarded partially by a continual posting of visible sentries. The husband and wife who say of one another, "I am my lover's and my lover is mine," (Song of Songs 6:3) say so not only to each other but to friends and coworkers and even strangers. By doing so, they stake out love's claim on their lives.

At the beginning of Solomon's Song of Songs, a young woman engaged to be married seeks such a public declaration from her lover.

> Tell me, you whom I love, where you graze your flock and where you rest your sheep at midday. Why should I be like a veiled woman beside the flocks of your friends? (1:7).

By access to her lover's plans for the day, the beloved sought an acknowledgment, visible to all her lover's friends and work companions, of her place in his life. She wanted to be able to visit him, openly and without embarrassment, in the chief places where his life was lived. By this access, love claimed dominion over work; it denied that there were rooms in the lover's heart where the beloved was not welcome. Of course, the beloved did not ask for a perpetual lovers' hideaway where work was permanently abandoned. Sheep require tending, and lovers require a livelihood. But she sought a love that wasn't ashamed of itself. She sought a love that touched all of her lover's life, even his work, and was not blocked off into some private placed and renounced elsewhere. She knew that in coming openly to see her lover and in being welcomed by him, the two were making a public testimony of their love for one another.

This witness to love is an important part of love's armor. It informs those with whom lovers have contact that each one's heart is already sealed. By the visible testimony of love, a husband and wife stake out love's claim on their lives. They warn others against attempting to set up camp in their hearts.

The kind of meeting described in the first chapter of Song of Songs is only one way lovers can declare their love publicly. They can also speak lovingly of one another in public. The great American lawyer and diplomat Joseph Choate was once asked at a dinner who he would prefer to be if he were not himself. Rather than name some celebrity of his day, Choate caught his wife's eye and replied, "If I could not be myself, I would like to be Mrs. Choate's second husband." We may not possess Choate's great wit, but we can nevertheless praise our spouses in public. I suspect that praise for my wife is most effective when she's not around to hear it. Then, those to whom I describe her know that I am not speaking well of her simply because she is hovering about. And Lee, if word gets back to her that I said something nice about her when she wasn't around, knows also that I needn't have done so had I not really meant what I said.

Whether at work or among friends, lovers can strengthen the defenses of their love by talking about one another in loving and appreciative terms. Here and there, I try to mention something appreciative about Lee to my colleagues and students. Doing so comes mostly natural to me, but even if it did not, I would concentrate on talking about her from time to time. I know that by making public my love and appreciation of her, I am staking love's claim in my life. Of course, speaking unfavorably of a spouse in public has exactly the opposite effect. No claim to love is staked. In fact, friends, colleagues, and even strangers may hear an invitation: "Love has no claim on this life, so feel free to stake one of your own."

Lovers who wish to announce their love to others should also develop the mannerisms of love when they are together in public. These mannerisms need not include the kind of passionate embraces and kisses that teenage sweethearts tend to indulge in. An arm around a waist will do instead, a smile from across a room, a momentary holding of hands. These subtle signals again testify to love's dominion over the lives of a husband and wife. Like a sticker on the window of a house that says, "Protected by Acme Alarm Company," these signals will guard love by discouraging some intruders.

Choosing a Different Street for Walking

Another aspect of the labor required to protect love can be found in Solomon's advice to his son in the fifth chapter of Proverbs. More than once in the book of Proverbs, Solomon warns his son about the awful consequences of succumbing to the temptation of the adulterous woman. A husband, he counsels his son, can no more commit adultery without suffering grave harm than he can scoop a fire into his lap without burning his clothes (6:27–29). The house of the adulteress "is a highway to the grave, leading down to the chambers of death" (7:27). In Proverbs 5, Solomon gives practical advice for avoiding ruin at the hands of the adulterous woman.

My son, pay attention to my wisdom, listen well to my words of insight, that you may maintain discretion and your lips may preserve knowledge. For the lips of the adulteress drip honey, and her speech is smoother than oil; but in the end she is bitter as gall, sharp as a double-edged sword. Her feet go down to death; her steps lead straight to the grave. She gives no thought to the way of life; her paths are crooked, but she knows it not. Now then, my sons, listen to me, do not turn aside from what I say. Keep to a path far from her, do not go near the door of her house. . . . (5:1–8a).

Solomon's wisdom is blunt and practical. To keep from being found in the bed of the adulterous woman, his son must keep himself far from her house; far even from her street. Resisting temptation is partly a matter of avoiding the street where temptation lives. We guard our hearts by keeping track of our feet. "God," Paul wrote to the church at Corinth, "will . . . provide a way out [of temptation] so that you can stand up under it" (1 Cor. 10:13). For many of us, however, the way out was two exits back.

We may be skeptical of Solomon on this point. "Surely there's nothing sinful about walking down a street or even past a particular house," someone will think. "What could be wrong with a perfectly innocent stroll?" These observations miss the point. Solomon was not interested with the morality of walking. He was, however, concerned that his son sees that the avoidance of temptation sometimes, perhaps even frequently, requires altering a pattern of otherwise innocent activities. The time to resist the temptation of sexual infidelity is not moments before the act.

Flirting with the adulterous man or woman is like lighting a stick of dynamite and then trying to blow out the fuse. Dag Hammarskjöld, the Swedish diplomat who served as Secretary General of the United Nations during the 1950s, wrote, "You cannot play with the animal in you without becoming wholly animal, play with falsehood without forfeiting your right to truth, play cruelty without losing your sensitivity of mind. He who wants to keep his garden tidy doesn't reserve a plot for weeds."[2]

How wide a berth does a particular temptation require? This depends largely on the magnitude of the temptation and the likelihood that we may succumb to it. For example, consider the temptation of sexual infidelity. The most cursory glance about us reveals, I think, that this particular temptation is great and that any one of us, given the right circumstances, could be snared by it. From King David, who committed adultery with Bathsheba, to contemporary church leaders, the list of those who have betrayed the vow of faithfulness is distressingly long. Shouldn't we conclude that strong measures are called for in this area? "So long as there are wild beasts about," George MacDonald once said, "It is better to be afraid than secure." Shouldn't we be more fearful about the possibility of infidelity? Shouldn't that fearfulness cause us to take greater precautions?

The most important practical step to be taken to avoid the temptation of sexual infidelity can be summed up in a simple rule: *Avoid spending time alone with anyone of the opposite sex.* We saw in an earlier chapter that the chief labor of love is the labor of making time for love. The key ingredient of almost any love, whether the faithful love of a husband and wife or the unfaithful love that betrays the marriage vow, is *time.*

Love is born out of time to grow familiar, time to speak and listen to the heart's secrets, time to watch one another, time to accumulate memories that cause two separate individuals to say "we." If you wish to deprive your heart of opportunity to fall in love with someone other than your spouse, you can take no more important step than to deprive your heart of the accumulated moments out of which such loves have their birth. Falling in love with another man or woman may seem like a sudden occurrence that takes a heart by surprise. In reality, this kind of love is rarely a sudden thing. It almost always grows out of shared conversations and lunches and tasks. Little by little the grip of faithful love is loosened, and the grasp of betraying love gains strength. You cannot give unfaithful love the time to grow without giving it birth and life.

In a previous chapter we asked where we might find time to build faithful love. We might as well be frank here about where unfaithful love will find time to take root and blossom. For men and women who work in an office environment, for example, time to build a love-betraying love is easy to come by: an hour spent at lunch talking about the office and then about more personal matters. An evening working frantically together on some project and then a late supper. Perhaps a business trip with shared breakfasts and taxis. But men and women need not be coworkers to find time for betraying love. Spending time running or playing tennis together will do as well as a business lunch. Regularly driving home alone together after church choir practice is as good as a business trip. Even the professional intimacy of the counseling environment can provide time enough for love to grow between a man and a woman pledged to other loves.

Faithful love has, then, ample reason to hedge itself about with barriers against private encounters with men other than a husband or women other than a wife. As a law professor, this means that I will forego lunches and racquetball games with my female students. It means that even with my female colleagues I will avoid all but group lunches.

There are, incidentally, strong reasons besides avoiding the temptation of unfaithfulness for men especially to be cautious in their relations with female coworkers or, in my case, students. Sexual harassment is, by at least some accounts, widespread in both job and educational environments. And the possibility of misinterpreted attentions or even false accusations is real. Thus, I make it a practice to keep my office door open when female students visit me for help in a course or for general advice. Similarly, Lee and I have tried to make it a practice for her to drive all baby-sitters home and for me to avoid dropping in at our house when a baby-sitter is looking after our children while Lee is out.

Are all these precautions really necessary? Is faithfulness really so fragile a thing as to require these extravagant protections? Perhaps not. I only know that purer hearts and more disciplined characters have betrayed love and their marriage partners. None of them intended to do so when they pledged perpetual fidelity. But they did nevertheless. And their unfaithfulness cost them marriages, sometimes careers, and always pain.

Recognizing Temptation

We guard love partially by learning to recognize the threats to love. What will the temptation to infidelity look like when it appears before us? We would be better off if we could learn to recognize temptation from a distance, before it breathes sweetly in our faces. Solomon, in fact, offers his son a fairly vivid description of temptation in chapter 7 of Proverbs, so that he will not be taken by surprise when its honeyed voice calls him by name.

> At the window of my house I looked out through the lattice. I saw among the simple, I noticed among the young men, a youth who lacked judgment. He was going down the street near [the adulteress'] corner, walking along in the direction of her house at twilight, as the day was fading, as the dark of night set in.

Then out came a woman to meet him, dressed like a prostitute and with crafty intent. (She is loud and defiant, her feet never stay at home; now in the street, now in the squares, at every corner she lurks.) She took hold of him and kissed him and with a brazen face she said:

"I have fellowship offerings at home; today I fulfilled my vows. So I came out to meet you; I looked for you and have found you! I have covered my bed with colored linens from Egypt. I have perfumed my bed with myrrh, aloes and cinnamon. Come, let's drink deep of love till morning; let's enjoy ourselves with love! My husband is not at home; he has gone on a long journey. He took his purse filled with money and will not be home till full moon."

With persuasive words she led him astray; she seduced him with her smooth talk. All at once he followed her like an ox going to the slaughter, like a deer stepping into a noose till an arrow pierces his liver, like a bird darting into a snare, little knowing it will cost him his life. (vv. 6–23).

Notice these elements of the adulteress' temptation.

The beginning

Before the adulteress ever spoke a word, or even cast an alluring glance in the direction of the young man, temptation was set in motion. It began when the man went "down the street near her corner, walking in the direction of her house." As we have seen before, one avoids infidelity partially by avoiding the places where it is likely to occur.

The hospitality of darkness

Darkness and secrecy are the familiar attendants of temptation. The private lunch, the evening at work alone together, the business trip to a distant city—these are the moments when temptation proposes what we would reject out of hand in other circumstances. "Food eaten in secret is delicious," Folly declares in Proverbs 9:17. The promise of secrecy is both the beginning and the end of the temptation in Proverbs 7. The gathering darkness is the first assurance of secrecy. And the final verbal tug the adulteress makes upon the young man is to give him an additional promise that their night will be undetected. "My husband is not at home; he has gone on a long journey. He took his purse filled with money and will not be home till full moon." Here is temptation's most effective pitch: "No one will know. No one will see."

The thrill of defiance

Temptation does not always come clothed in brazenness, but here in Proverbs 7 it does. The adulteress attacks first with a bold and flamboyant approach. She comes out to meet the young man, dressed as a prostitute, loud and defiant, brazen-faced, clutching the youth's hand and kissing him. For this man, directness does the trick that demureness might accomplish with another.

The attraction of attention

According to the adulteress, her encounter with the young man is not accidental. "I came out to meet you," she says, "I looked for you and have found you." There is in all of us the desire to found by someone, to be the object of someone else's search, a treasure sought for and finally discovered. The adulteress touches the young man with the tangible caress of attention. She conveys to him that he has suddenly moved from the periphery of innumerable visions to the center of her own.

The promise of extraordinary pleasure

The adulteress lures the youth with the prospect of novel pleasure. She does not offer yesterday's warmed-over lamb to satisfy his hunger, but fellowship offerings, the portion of an offering that the offerer could eat as part of the sacrificial celebration. Ironically, the night of sin with the adulteress will begin with what is essentially a religious feast. By feasting first on the fellowship offerings, the adulterous pair cloak their sin with the garb of holiness, as if what they are about to do is not so bad that they cannot pray before doing it.

The special meal is followed by an invitation to an exotic bed covered with linens from Egypt, perfumed with myrrh, aloes, and cinnamon. For one night the youth steps out of the hum-drum routine of the work-a-day world and feasts his senses on what he could otherwise only partake of in fantasy. A fancy meal, an exotic bed, a woman brazenly erotic.

The scene Solomon describes is intended to give his son advance warning of temptation, so that he may see it coming at a distance, and seeing, avoid it. The temptation to infidelity may come in forms as varied as our weaknesses. And so, Solomon's description should be taken only as one possible scenario of temptation. But at least certain elements of the picture Solomon paints are probably very common strands in the web of temptation.

We are probably most vulnerable to the temptation of infidelity when alone with someone of the opposite sex in private circumstances, just as the temptation in Proverbs 7 occurs during hours of darkness when the husband is away on a business trip. Moreover, the temptation to infidelity is probably accompanied frequently by a special attentiveness in someone of the opposite sex, an attention we may be starved for in our own marriages. And finally, the mere allure of novelty, of Egyptian linens or their modern counterparts, is a strong element in most sexual temptation.

Imagining a Bitter End

In Proverbs 5, Solomon seeks to guard his son from the bitter fruit of adultery in another way. He calls upon him to participate in a kind of antifantasy. He may have already imagined the adulterous woman in his mind. He may have seen her alluring clothes and removed them. Perhaps he smelled the musky sweetness of her perfume and slid his hands across the satin silkiness of the sheets on her bed. Solomon's son may have caressed these imaginations in his mind in idle moments. And each time the young man allowed these fantasies to captivate his mind, the siren call of the adulteress became a little more audible, the pleasant thought of walking down her street a little more irresistible.

Solomon advises his son to entertain a different fantasy, however. This one is far less pleasant, more like a nightmare that wakes a sleeper with a cold sweat. Instead of perfume and silk, Solomon challenged his son to imagine the destruction he would reap at the hands of the adulterous woman.

> Now then . . . listen to me; do not turn aside from what I say. Keep to a path far from her, do not go near the door of her house, lest you give your best strength to others and your years to one who is cruel, least strangers feast on your wealth and your toil enrich another man's house. At the end of your life you will groan, when your flesh and body are spent. You will say, "How I hated discipline! How my heart spurned correction! I would not obey my teachers or listen to my instructors. I have come to the brink of utter ruin in the midst of the assembly" (Prov. 5:7–14).

Here, then, is another strategy for guarding love against unfaithfulness. Periodically focus your mind not on the imagined pleasure of infidelity but on its inevitable loss. Imagine bitter weeping, pain that will not relent, and loneliness so tangible that you can feel its breath upon your face. Imagine your children learning to call another man, "father," or another woman, "mother." Imagine Christmas and birthdays without them. Imagine yourself alone late at night, the images of a television screen washing across your face but not bringing ease to your heart.

Part of the greatness of a great writer like Leo Tolstoy is the ability to help us imagine possible futures. In *Anna Karenina* Tolstoy opens a window on the bitter fruit of infidelity by describing the moments immediately following the first physical consummation of Anna's adulterous affair with Count Vronsky.

That which to Vronsky had been for almost a whole year the one absorbing desire of his life, replacing all his old desires; that which to Anna had been an impossible, terrible, and, for that very reason, a more entrancing dream of happiness—that desire had been fulfilled. He stood before her, pale, his lower jaw quivering, and besought her to be calm, without himself knowing how or why.

"Anna! Anna!" he said with a quivering voice, "Anna, for God's sake! . . ."

But the louder he spoke, the lower she cast down her once proud and gay, but now shame-stricken head, and she bowed down and sank from the sofa where she was sitting—down on the floor, at his feet; she would have fallen on the carpet if he had not held her.

"My God! Forgive me!" she said, sobbing, pressing his hands to her bosom.

She felt so sinful, so guilty, that nothing was left her but to humiliate herself and beg forgiveness, and as now there was no one in her life but him, to him, too, she addressed her prayer for forgiveness. Looking at him, she had a physical sense of her humiliation, and she could say nothing more. And he felt as a murderer must feel when he beholds the body he has robbed of life. That body, robbed by him of life, was their love, the first state of their love. There was something awful and revolting in the memory of what had been bought at this fearful price of shame. Shame at her spiritual nakedness crushed her and infected him. But in spite of all the murderer's horror before the body of the victim, he must hack it to pieces, hide the body, must use what the murderer had gained by his murder.

And as the murderer, with fury, and, as it were, with passion, falls on the body, and drags it, and hacks at it—so he covered her face and shoulders with kisses. She held his hand, and did not stir. Yes, these kisses—that is what has been bought by this shame. Yes, and this one hand, which will always be mine—the hand of my accomplice. She lifted up that hand and kissed it. He sank on his knees and tried to see her face; but she hid it, and said nothing. At last, as though making an effort over herself, she got up and pushed him away. Her face was still as beautiful, but it was only the more pitiful for that.

"All is over," she said; "I have nothing but you. Remember that."

"I can never forget what is my whole life. For one instant of this happiness . . ."

"Happiness!" she said with horror and loathing and her horror unconsciously infected him. "For God's sake, not a word, not a word more."

She rose quickly and moved away from him.

"Not a word more," she repeated, and with a look of chill despair, incomprehensible to him, she parted from him.[3]

Would you or I rush forward to embrace such a future? Of course not. We would do everything in our power to choose happiness over such pain. We would sacrifice momentary pleasure for lasting good for ourselves, our husbands or wives, and our children. So Solomon bids us look into the possible future and order our lives according to what we see in our imagination but never wish to see in reality. We may grasp the fruit of infidelity and bite deeply into its rottenness, or we may look before we eat of it and cast it aside. One day it will be too late to declare, "If only I had seen where this path would lead." Solomon tells us that we can see now, if only we will, and choose a better path.

The Threat of Emptiness

Love thrives on life. It can prevail over adversity and want, survive in the face of pain and bitter loss. But it cannot endure the death rattle of life that has ceased to be life.

Sometimes infidelity is the desperate gasp of an individual looking for a way out of an aimless and empty life. The heart, starved of meaning, looks for it in the arms of another man or woman. Those who have been numbed by an endless succession of empty days are overcome by a sudden passion and drink it in, like desert wanderers who haven't seen water for miles.

The passion that temporarily rescues a life from tedium never proves permanent, and emptiness invariably returns to find a roomy apartment. But the starving are rarely picky eaters, and the combination of emptiness and sudden passion will typically prove to be an irresistible temptation to betray love. We guard love from this kind of infidelity by taking care to guard our lives from the emptiness that nourishes it.

Each soul has its own personal fear, one that lies close to the heart and makes the pulse pound in the dark. Perhaps a man or woman fears financial ruin or being passed over for advancement at work. But there are greater evils than these lurking about. Those who aspire to lasting love must learn to fear emptiness. We should fear inhabiting life rather than living it, occupying a place rather than filling it. We should fear the life spent in the flickering shadow of television and cinema. We should dread leaving behind a sentence in a newspaper that says, "He has left closets full of books but a life devoid of significant events; he bequeaths to his wife and children an inheritance of empty days."

We cannot pour our lives into emptiness without becoming empty ourselves. We cannot tip a cistern over and allow the water to splash against dry, parched ground without losing it. "They followed worthless idols," the prophet Jeremiah recorded, "and became worthless themselves" (2:5b). We can always have plenty of nothing. It lies near at hand and in great abundance. Empty books and television programs and movies mesmerize us with nothingness. And we pour ourselves into them and are molded into the form of their emptiness. Nothing, C. S. Lewis once wrote, is very strong,

> strong enough to steal away a man's best years not in sweet sins but in a dreary flickering of the mind over it knows not what and knows not why, in the gratification of curiosities so feeble that the man is only half aware of them, in drumming of fingers and kicking of heels, in whistling tunes that he does not like, or in the long, dim labyrinth of reveries that have not even lust or ambition to give them a relish. . . .[4]

If we attend closely enough, we will almost surely feel the clutch and grab of a thousand hands that would tie us to a couch or an easy chair. There are clogs for the brain as well as the blood—drugs and drink and food and TV, a mind-numbing grab bag of ways to fill a life with empty space.

For those trapped in the web of empty life, an affair sometimes looks like a way out. And so, those who would protect love from unfaithfulness must protect it from the clutch of emptiness.

> You can strangle love with boredom as surely as you can poison it with infidelity.

I should hasten to add, though, that not everyone who feels they have an empty life has an affair. A husband and wife who have slipped into a life devoid of purpose and meaning may never betray one another with some other lover. But they have betrayed love, nevertheless, because they let it die. For every marriage that explodes in the face of adultery, another dissolves in the face of unremitting emptiness, "not with a bang," as T. S. Eliot wrote, "but a whimper." Love can survive pain and trouble and lifelong toil. But it cannot survive emptiness. You can strangle love with boredom as surely as you can poison it with infidelity. A love that lasts a lifetime requires life, real life, abundant life. You can build no sturdier defense for love than to reinforce it with life.

Those who follow the Risen Christ should be the world's greatest lovers, because their love shares the fire of the abundant life to which Christ has called them. "I have come," Jesus said of His followers, "that they may have life, and have it to the full" (John 10:10). The fruit that Christ produces in the lives of those in whom His Spirit dwells—love, joy, peace, patience, kindness, goodness, faithfulness, gentleness and self-control (Gal. 5:22)—is the nourishment that lasting love thrives on. So if you would secure love, fasten it to a life lived in pursuit of Christ.

1. William Law, *A Serious Call to a Devout and Holy Life* (Philadelphia: The Westminster Press), 22.
2. Dag Hammarskjöld, *Markings*, trans. Leif Sjöberg and W. H. Auden (New York: Ballantine), 9.

3. Leo Tolstoy, *Anna Karenina*, trans. Bernard Guilbert Guerney (Norwalk, Conn.: The Easton Press), 172–73.

4. C. S. Lewis, *The Screwtape Letters*, (New York: MacMillan, 1961), 64.

9

Guarding Love from Transferred Delight

*T*he common picture of a middle-aged marriage is one in which the wife has gradually built her life around her children and various social groups and the husband in turn has built his life around a career and Monday night football. Each has found delight in something besides the other. They did not do so all at once, of course. There was a time when they preferred each other's company to anyone else's, when the secrets they shared together were the most important secrets. But gradually they transferred delight in one another to new things. They came to find their chief identity and joy in careers, perhaps, and little by little evenings and weekends together became a tedious interlude between the frantic but fulfilling days of work. Or perhaps they cultivated different hobbies, and what began as minor diversions became consuming passions not shared by their lover.

This transfer of delight from spouse to other things will inevitably spell the death of love. Love must be guarded against the theft of delight. There is nothing wrong with work or hobbies. But if allowed to become a principal source of delight, they steal delight from love. And a love that produces no delight—no joy—is a love that is dying or dead.

So how do we protect love from the transfer of delight? How do we see that it keeps on gushing forth joy like a Texas oil well perched on top of an inexhaustible reservoir of liquid gold?

Recall again Solomon's advice in Proverbs 5. After he counseled his son to keep his steps far from the path of infidelity, Solomon encouraged him to make faithful love the focus of his attention.

> Find joy with the wife you married in your youth, fair as a hind, graceful as a fawn. Let hers be the company you keep, hers the breasts that ever fill you with delight, hers the love that ever holds you captive (5:18–19).

Solomon instructed his son to "find joy" with the wife of his youth. What are we to make of this seemingly crazy suggestion that we can somehow determine where we will find joy and delight? We are used to thinking that happiness and joy are things beyond our control, blessings that pierce our lives with sweetness at unforeseen moments that we cannot predict and can only long for.

But Scripture differs from our everyday thinking precisely at this point. The Bible teaches that we can choose the focus of our joy and the objects of our delight. It commands us, for example, to delight ourselves in the Lord. "Delight yourself in the LORD and he will give you the desires of your heart," the psalmist wrote (37:4). Those who delight themselves in the law of the Lord are promised blessing (Ps. 1:1–2). By these commands and promises God seems to be calling upon us to reevaluate our notions of joy. We are to see that joy is not something that lands upon us unexpectedly but something that we seek in particular places. And when we seek joy in the right places, the Scripture promises us that we will find it.

For husbands and wives, the Bible commands that joy and delight be sought in one another. But how do we do this? *Chiefly by seeing to it that we reserve both energy and interest for our beloved and for the work of love.*

It has generally been my experience that the things I seek after enthusiastically will eventually become objects of delight for me. I think I first discovered this truth when I decided to learn how to play the guitar. When I was in the sixth grade, I discovered an old guitar in the back of a closet in our house that my father had gotten in trade for an electric motor. I bought a book about playing the guitar and started practicing. Actually, I started experiencing pain and exasperation. For weeks my fingers ached from the contortion of trying to bend them into the shape of chords. How I cursed the F-chord! *Three* awkward and aching fingers had to press *four* strings against the guitar frets. Until I had practiced long enough to earn callouses, the guitar strings dug creases in my fingers. For weeks my hands refused to work together. I could make a chord with the fingers of one hand or strum a rhythm with the fingers of the other hand but not do both at the same time. I raged, but I kept practicing. One day the chords began to sound like folk music, and I have been a guitar player ever since. Now, were I banished from civilization, along with a Bible and an armful of books, my guitar would accompany me into exile. It is almost like an arm or leg. It speaks joy to me.

What I discovered about the guitar I also discovered about countless other things. There is hardly a thing that I have ever thrown myself into that has not become a source of delight: the guitar, Tolstoy's *Anna Karenina*, the law, and my marriage with Lee.

Joy-producing love requires nothing more extravagant than time and energy. Like a fire, it needs tending with fuel, and it will generate delight. Marriages that do not produce delight, but only boredom, are marriages that have been robbed of time and energy. The attention of lovers has been transferred from their love to careers and hobbies, children and even churches, at the expense of delight.

But, you may ask, aren't careers necessary? Don't children have to be raised? Aren't church activities important? Of course. Lovers need not abandon work or children or ministries or friends in order to reap joy from their love. They must, however, resist allowing any of these activities to become the chief source of their delight. Lovers do this, to a large degree, by turning as many aspects of their lives as possible into joint enterprises. The care of children, for example, with all its attendant delights, ought to be filtered through the lives of both lovers together. In this way the delight produced by children remains entwined with the delight of love itself. "See what our love has wrought?" the lovers ask one another. Children become a source of transferred delight when they are more "*our* children" than "*my* children."

What, then, of a career? I confess to having grave reservations about the very word "career." It seems to resonate with a meaning inconsistent with the biblical idea of marriage as two becoming one flesh. A career is a path, a trajectory, a history. But it is traveled and lived by only a single person. One speaks of "my career," or perhaps "our *careers*," but never of "our *career*." We ought to be suspicious that something unhealthy to love lurks behind these ordinary expressions.

Older words displaced by the notion of a "career" were more consistent with the labor required by love. "Vocation," for instance, means a calling and reflects the idea that work arises out of God's calling of a worker or workers to particular work. Vocation, then, suggests a balanced triangle of Caller, called, and calling, rather than the self-centered idea of a career. Even the less glamorous word "work" is more hospitable to love's labor than "career." It suggest less of the self-consuming aspect of a career and leaves open the possibility of "works," rather than the narrow notion of a single life-embracing "work."

Whatever word we use to speak of the labor that earns lovers money to sustain life, we cannot be too careful to avoid the seduction of all that "career" now stands for. Whether pursued by a wife or a husband or by both, career advancement threatens to unravel the cord of love and substitute for it separate threads leading off in separate directions. How do we prevent this unraveling?

First, we can resist the temptation to define ourselves and the multifaceted work to which we are called by something so narrow as a career. Perhaps we should begin by frustrating the information gatherers who are always calling upon us to fill in a blank after the word, "occupation." Should we not respond by listing the callings that occupy our time: follower of Christ, husband, father, law professor. Why should we dignify the godlike claims of career over our self-identities? Why should we satisfy the narrow minds that desire to strip us of the rich tangle of callings to which God bids us?

Second, lovers committed to the lifetime labor of love and of realizing the two-become-oneness that God has substituted for their former singleness should treat occupations as joint property and common endeavors. I have tried, for example, to think of my work—first as an attorney and now as a law professor—as though I were an employee of the relationship that God has crafted of Lee and me. Both figuratively and in fact I ask Lee, "What shall we do with my earning ability for the next year or so?" This was exactly the question we wrestled with in 1988 when we considered whether I should leave the practice of law to teach at a law school. My work as an attorney both brought good things to our relationship and detracted from it. It brought us money—more than any other work I seemed suited for. Moreover, because I enjoyed the work and was good at it, I came home happier and more satisfied than I might have been coming home from other work. But, as I wrote in an earlier chapter, my work as an attorney subtracted important things from our love: time and peace.

We ultimately looked hard at my work as an attorney and decided that it was too expensive for our love, that it cost us more than it earned. The Father was gracious in providing us with an alternative—teaching—that I would enjoy as much, and in many ways more, than the practice of law. I will be frank and say that I don't know what we would have done had we been forced to choose between work that I enjoyed and work that I found tedious or boring. I do not think my happiness or fulfillment at work should have been allowed to trump all other considerations pertinent to our love. It is one thing among others to take into account.

Even after I became a law professor, our joint consultations about my earning work continued. Would I concentrate my study and teaching and writing in the business and commercial subjects that would increase my opportunities for career advancement as a professor of law, or would I focus on less "marketable" subjects that interested me more? We chose the latter. Having once given up a path that would have produced the most money, it wasn't difficult to do it again. And so today I spend the bulk of my time writing and studying about church/state legal issues and legal ethics. I mention this decision only because it was again a joint deliberation and a decision in which both Lee and I participated.

Careers, though, are not the only thefts of the delight that love should produce. Ministries and hobbies may become sources of transferred delight as well. How do we frustrate this occurrence?

Again, the key to sustaining love's capacity to delight is to resist the drift toward separateness in ministries and hobbies, as well as in careers. Lovers must jointly supervise their individual ministries and sources of recreation. They will, in the first place, be cautious of committing too much of their time to separate activities. Their primary earning or home-sustaining labor will already commit them to largely separate days. The labor of talking and listening can help to forge oneness even out of these separate labors, but even this labor of intimacy may prove insufficient to bridge the gap between lives persistently lived apart as separate ministries and recreations are added to separate days of work. Lee and I have tried to find ministry and recreation together whenever possible. I have avoided diversions such as golf, for example, because they require more time than we believe our labor of love can spare. This attempt at togetherness helps to eliminate possible sources of transferred delight since it is hard to transfer my delight in our love to things that our love embraces together.

In our case, this labor calls for continued wrestling over the allotment of love's time and energy we make to separate pursuits. This work is not easy and has generated its share of conflict.

Lee, for example, for a while operated a part-time business teaching and managing aerobic dance classes in our community. She is good at this work and finds in it an outlet for her gifts. But like all work, hers takes time—time I can't share. She must learn the aerobic dance routines, keep track of a variety of business records, teach the classes, and try to keep the classes full by contacting students by telephone and letter. We have not infrequent discussions, and (I will be honest) not infrequent disagreements, about how Lee should structure this work so that it does not claim too great a share of the time that is our love's principal asset.

I, on the other hand, am presently laboring to write this book. For the last few weeks, as I wrote these words, I have spent about two hours every evening on our porch, boombox resonating with classic music or jazz, trying to pry the words out of my head and onto yellow legal pads. Some of the time Lee can spend with me, and my work is punctuated by talk with her. But she has work of her own inside the house, and sometimes, even when she does not, she does not tolerate the bugs of a Mississippi summer as well as I do. So we are apart.

We battle against separateness even at this point. Since this is a book partially about our love, Lee is a regular consultant to and critic of the writing. It is partially her voice that speaks here. Even when she does not actively talk with me about the contents of particular chapters, I try to consult her regularly about the time the writing is taking. Is she still comfortable with the time we have given over for me to finish this book? Should we rearrange things tonight to spend more time together? When can she come out onto the porch? If the bugs are a problem, then perhaps when she is through with the work she is doing, I can drag my yellow pad to the computer for typing and she can sit in the green chair with a book or letters to write, and we can talk as I type and she reads or writes.

It is even possible to transfer delight from the partner God has joined us with to "holy" things. We must tread cautiously at this point. It is not possible to overlove God or to focus too much on pleasing Him. Christ pressed this point to the limits of vividness when He told a crowd of people following Him one day: "If anyone comes to me and does not hate his father and mother, his wife and children, his brothers and sisters—yes, even his own life—he cannot be my disciple"

(Luke 14:26). Christ, the great Hound of Heaven, is the relentless pursuer of the hearts of men and women. He cannot be bought off with any tribute less than the heart's full devotion. The first and greatest commandment was, and is, "Love the Lord your God with all your heart and with all your soul and with all your mind" (Matt. 22:37). It was in obedience to this command that Temple Gairdner prayed:

> That I may come near to her, draw me nearer to thee than to her; that I may know her, make me to know thee more than her; that I may love her with the perfect love of a perfectly whole heart, cause me to love thee more than her and most of all. Amen. Amen. That nothing may be between me and her, be thou between us, every moment. That we may be constantly together, draw us into separate loneliness with thyself. And when we meet breast to breast, my God, let it be on thine own. Amen. Amen.[1]

As we love the Lord with all that we are, He enlarges our capacity to love, as if the love launched by the soul to God is then reflected back on the objects of our world. The second command, Jesus said, is to love neighbors as ourselves (Matt. 22:39). Later, the apostle Paul included in this list of reflected loves the love of a husband for his wife, a command, in fact, for husbands to love their wives "as Christ loved the church." Having captured our love, God sends the prisoner back to do the work of His bidding in the form of loving neighbors, wives, husbands, children, and enemies.

Married love is a love that produces . . .
a delight holy enough for the most
devout saint to find joy in.

The great mistake of many outwardly religious people is to imagine that love for God will always find expression in "pious" works—church attendance, almsgiving to the poor, choir practices, and Bible studies. But the string of "holy" activities that causes a man or woman to neglect spouse and children and neighbors nearby is a sure sign of a heart that has not been wholly captured, perhaps not captured at all, by God.

The one who has not loved the people God has assigned us as objects of love has not loved God. "[A]nyone who does not love his brother whom he has seen," the apostle John wrote, "cannot love God, whom he has not seen" (1 John 4:20b). The German pastor and theologian Dietrich Bonhoeffer once made a similar point.

> I believe that we ought so to love and trust God in our *lives*, and in all the good things that he sends us, that when the time comes (but not before!) we may go to him with love, trust, and joy. But, to put it plainly, for a man in his wife's arms to be hankering after the other world is, in mild terms, a piece of bad taste, and not God's will. We ought to find and love God in what he actually gives us; if it pleases him to allow us to enjoy some overwhelming earthly happiness, we mustn't try to be more pious than God himself and allow our happiness to be corrupted by presumption and arrogance, and by unbridled religious fantasy which is never satisfied with what God gives. God will see to it that the man who finds him in his earthly happiness and thanks him for it does not lack reminder that heart to what is eternal, and that sooner or later there will be times when he can say in all sincerity, "I wish I were home." But everything has its time, and the main thing is that we keep step with God, and do not keep pressing on a few steps ahead—nor keep dawdling a step behind.[2]

Married love *is* a holy love, because a holy God has chosen for men and women who have loved Him without reservation to see that love reflected back at least partially in a love for one another. Married love is a love that produces delight, a delight holy enough for the most devout saint to find joy in.

There is nothing easy or free of irritation in our labor to preserve love from the transfer of delight. I am frequently rankled by the time Lee's aerobic classes consume, she of the time I sit lost in a book or a pad of paper or a computer screen. We grate against one another sometimes. But love survives as a joy-giving flame because we will not, we must not, let it go out.

1. The Oxford Book of Prayers, ed. George Appleton (New York: MacMillan, 1961), 114.
2. Dietrich Bonhoeffer, *Letters and Papers from Prison*, ed. Eberhard Bethge (New York: Collier Books, 1972), 168–69.

Conclusion

few years ago a winter ice storm descended on northern Mississippi where we live. The temperature dropped suddenly and turned the water that had soaked the trees into ice. As night wore on, branches began to splinter with the weight of ice. Water in the trees expanded upwards and eventually caused the topmost tips of the trees to explode with a loud crack. The combined reports of these explosions sounded like a war zone. Electric wires collapsed under the weight of ice and falling branches, and most of the houses in our area were clothed in darkness—without light or heat.

The next morning I ventured outside and discovered that my yard, normally canopied by a dozen large trees, was a jumble of fallen branches and one fallen tree. Over the next few days, I set to the task of cutting up the fallen branches and tree with a chain saw.

My son, Ben, was about eight years old at the time. After I had finished cutting up the wood, I stacked the larger pieces to be burned later in our wood stove but left most of the smaller pieces for Ben to pick up and stack. There was probably enough wood left to occupy a grown man a couple of hours, working diligently. I told Ben that I would pay him for gathering the remaining pieces of wood and stacking them up. He was happy at the thought of having some money to spend and quickly began gathering up the pieces. But within a few minutes his enthusiasm waned and his mind turned to play. It eventually took Ben a couple of weeks to finish the job. I had to prod him constantly to stop playing and concentrate on the task. "Keep at it, son," I said to my boy, and as I said those words, I heard them rising up as an echo out of my own childhood.

When I was a teenager, my family lived in a house surrounded by more than five acres of yard on Moses Lake, near Galveston, Texas. The job of cutting the grass during the summer months was mine, and each week I spent ten or twelve hours making circuits of the lawn on a riding lawnmower. For hours I wheeled around tallow tree saplings, spraying clippings of St. Augustine grass in my wake. Occasionally, I stopped to add gas to the mower and sometimes dawdled before attacking the yard again. My father, normally at work on some project of his own around our house, would invariably remind me that the sun would be going down before I knew it. "Keep at it, son," was his standard admonition.

My images of life took shape partially in those long Saturdays as I made the long circuits around the yard at Moses Lake. The work was long. No matter how badly I wanted to be done with it, I couldn't by any amount of effort finish it quickly. The morning when the lawn mower first roared to life was always impossibly distant from the evening when the final strip of grass fell before the blades. No amount of adrenaline or effort could transform the long hours into mere minutes. I could only start the work and keep at it. Only later would I discover that most of life's important labors require perseverance as much as effort.

The labor of love is a long work, probably the longest work that any of us will ever undertake. I have labored at loving my wife Lee longer than I have labored to learn the law or practice it or teach it. My professional careers as an attorney and law professor are like brief interludes compared with the years spanned by my love for Lee. And I will, if God grants me life long enough, one day retire from those careers even as I continue my career of love for her.

I wonder sometimes whether love's labor has suffered in this generation because we have collectively lost touch with lifetime lasting labors. We change jobs regularly, change careers even. We find ourselves constantly adjusting to new employers, ever ready to send out résumés if a new job doesn't work out.

Love's calling, though, is to a long labor, one with no thought of relocation or promotion or better compensation package. You can't reduce love's labor to a brief entry in a pocket calendar—it is meant to consume a whole life. You can't charge into love's labor during the early days after the honeymoon and expect to finish the job quickly and then move on to other projects.

Men especially may stumble at this news. Of course they plan to love their wives for a lifetime. But they are accustomed to thinking of life as a series of jobs to be tackled energetically one at a time, completed, and then left behind as some new work becomes the object of attention. They stand back with satisfaction at the completion of some job and smile with contentment. "Finished! Now, what's next?"

It may come hard, then, to see love as work that never gets finished. But you will not last through the long years of love's labor without understanding this. You must turn to it again every morning. Love is not a trophy to be won but a lifetime to be lived. You can't finish the job quickly just by pitching in energetically from time to time. Love requires energy, of course, but a sustained energy. Sometimes the work is exhilarating and you scarce think of love as labor at all, but sometimes it is hard and requires patience and endurance as much as enthusiasm. Often the work is almost routine, like the steady roar of the riding lawnmower on long summer days around a lawn. You simply have to keep at it. Love keeps talking, keeps struggling to make time for one another in the rich tumble and confusion of life, keeps sharing secrets. Love never offers its laborers the possibility of an early retirement—or of any retirement. The labor of love is making time for love, talking and listening, sustaining intimacy, courtesy, acceptance, avoiding and resolving conflicts, and guarding love. This is not a checklist to complete but a lifetime to live.

Although the labor of love is long work that requires a life's best energy, it is anything but drudgery. Ultimately, I think those who finish the full course of love will be amazed that a lifetime of love could seem so short.

I lie awake sometimes at night, watching my beloved sleep, and I marvel at how quickly the years of our love's labor have passed so far. She exhales with a quiet whisper, and each escaping breath seems like another year passed. It was barely yesterday that I saw her for the first time, sitting in the front seat of a friend's car, long hair streaming. Now almost twenty years later I lie beside her, and like Jacob in the Old Testament who worked years for Rachel's father to win the right to marry her, the years seem only like a few days.